Mysterious stones of Mouselow – found on Castle Hill near Glossop

*Cover painting of Torside Castle and text illustrations
by artist David Kelsall*

Moor Mysteries

Copyright: Steve Cliffe 2021
Published by S.H.Publications 2021
ISBN 978-0-9514611-5-0

SH Publications

Moor Mysteries
Introduction

The vast untamed uplands darkly dominating the gap between the conurbations of Manchester and Yorkshire are sprinkled with names giving clues to their unforgiving nature – Black Hill, Bleaklow, Upper Dead Edge, Madwoman's Stones, Devil's Dyke and Kinder Downfall. They are also scattered with the mysterious wrecks of scores of aircraft, victims of weather conditions and navigational error and the undiscovered bog bodies of many a wayfarer who went astray. Step off the well-trodden path amongst these trackless peat bogs and it is easy to lose one's way.

But it is a mistake to imagine that these lands around the Peak District of Derbyshire have never been cultivated. Once, long ago – in a time far beyond the memory of recorded history, but within the last five millennia, Neolithic and Bronze Age people cultivated strip fields high up on what is now heather-clad moor in a period when the climate was warmer than today. They left substantial evidence of their houses, farming methods, circle temples, and even their tombs, before cooler wetter conditions drove them to seek sustenance in the valleys below the exposed moorland.

The wild moors of peat bog took millennia to form, clothed in coarse tussock grass, heather and ling, which bloom in brief purple glory in late summer, interspersed with the acid rain-stained dark gritstone rocks, rising like grounded battleships in a sea of peat. It is these gritstone and shale rocks, impervious to water, which give the area the name of the Dark Peak – a place waterlogged for most of the year and a breeding ground for peat creating mosses.

They are still managed by farmers and game wardens. Sheep graze here, grouse are raised for the lucrative shooting season and native species like the mountain hare, which changes its thick furry coat to miry white in the winter snow flurries, nibbles at the young shoots of heather and savours the mountain herb, whilst keeping an eye cocked for buzzard and hawk. It has seen strange things come and go, will o' th' wisps – otherworldly lights some would say. More recently it has seen the bearded vulture, a nightmare incomer from the French Alps with a nine foot wingspan which swallows the bones of dead sheep whole.

Peak Park rangers patrol the hillsides. They look after the paths, assist walkers and repair the gates, plant plugs of cotton grass and sow sphagnum moss to help consolidate depleted banks of peat, washed, eroded and burned away, which it is thought lock up a considerable amount of the earth's store of carbon. Sometimes in deep gulleys in the bogs, where winter rains uncovered them to glitter in the sun after thousands of years hidden in dark clammy peat, are found remains of ancient cultures – flint tools and weapons of the Mesolithic hunter-gatherers who pursued now extinct animals through trackless forests, to the sound of wildlife unfamiliar today.

Against this background of varied human usage the high moors boast strange phenomena which folk custom adds to the story of the place. Before the age of properly surfaced roads this area was exceedingly wild and inaccessible. No wonder it spawned legends. Even now it is riddled with routes which peter out over the wildest moors ending in stony tracks and boggy paths. This is one of the wild places of Britain.

One rocky road is the route up from Hayfield past Edale Cross and Kinder Low End, heading down Jacobs Ladder to Edale, one of the Peak's remotest valleys.

Legend tells that once a Templar knight did penance here for some misdeed, expiating his wickedness by helping medieval travellers cross the inhospitable terrain. A nearby rugged cave in the hillside was his shelter on stormy days. Today this spot is accessible to the public only on foot. And that has been the appeal of the place to millions of walkers since it was opened up to public access. A sense of timeless mystery and the space to breathe pervade the sweeping vistas.

As late as the 1940s Kinder Scout was off limits to hikers and only trespassers who braved gamekeepers could penetrate the hidden recesses. By Victorian times the moors were exerting an allure and fascination for a new breed of hiker, climber and caver, who set out with rucksack, rope and compass, clad prosaically in tweed suit, cap, and hobnail boots.

One was Ernest Baker, secretary of the outdoor adventure Kyndwr Club, who in 1900 wrote:

"A heathery moor wears the same impassible face it wore when Britain was peopled by savages. Perhaps these austere landscapes exercise a tonic influence upon our pampered and jaded minds – the physical sense of space and freedom; the suggestion of the mysterious and illimitable with which the shadowy expanses and dark ravines sway the imagination, as with the suggestiveness of poetry; true it is that the gloomy scenes which our grandfathers hated, draw us with a subtle and a powerful spell."

Baker usually carried a letter from the landowner authorising himself and companions to access the hillsides. But occasionally their excursions were enlivened by the absence of this passport to roam and the fun of evading the numerous keepers. In the 1930s this exploded in the Mass Trespass when a running fight between keepers and hikers took place resulting in prison sentences for some.

By the 1950s the Pennine Way legally opened the Kinder plateau to walkers and a writer of the time Nellie Kirkham commented:

"Other moors are wild and lonely, but Kinder has a desolation, an isolation, all its own; a desolation that is in no way depressing, but stimulating in its savagery. When you stand in the centre of the plateau you feel an immeasurable distance from anywhere. No matter where you turn there is nothing but sky and dark peat bog ranging from dark brown to black, worn down into channels up to fifteen feet deep. The stream beds at the bottom are silver sand, shining white pebbles, and gritstone blocks. There is practically no vegetation; here and there yards apart, are sparse clumps of tawny grass, but you can go a mile without seeing even a foot-wide clump of heather or bilberry. You begin to wonder whether there was ever anything else in the world."

This book navigates treacherous bogs to probe ancient lore and elusive Bleaklow leys and lights, the intriguing legends of caves on Kinder Scout, Roman soldiers, Templar knights, and the troglodytes and monsters of the adjoining 'hollow country' - such as "The Terror of Blue John Gap."

It is seventy years since The Peak became Britain's first national park. While legends fascinate the minds and imagination of quite sane ordinary people, some believe that these Peakland hills exert their mysterious power and strange manifestations are seen. The moors of Central England are the wildest places in the heart of Britain – a wilderness easily accessible to the largest number of people, and likely to remain so.

Steve Cliffe – June 2021

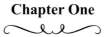

Chapter One

Legends of Longdendale

On the heathy moors and the great still hills the scurrying clouds, the open bleakness and the clear bright air thrills with vague energies and hope. Life, like the landscape around us, seems bigger wider and freer, a rainbow road leading to unknown ends

Jerome K. Jerome

Frontispiece from Middleton's book, 1900

At the end of the Victorian era local historian, Thomas Middleton, published his *Legends of Longdendale* a compilation of folklore acquired from old residents and existing sources with stories of ghosts wizards and tales of derring-do, but slight mention of the famous "Longdendale Lights" which appear to be a mainly late 20th century phenomena, and have not been seen at all in this present digital age,(excluding the inevitable aircraft landing lights) yet when anyone with a smartphone is a competent photographer and film maker.

Despite allusions to the tramp of ghostly Romans in references to the Lights in more recent literature and the actual existence of a least one likely Roman trackway and a Roman fort at Melandra near Glossop, Middleton never attempted to link the Roman presence with strange goings on across the moors above Longdendale. He also never mentioned the Devil's bonfires which local people are said to have seen over the moors.

He did mention an unearthly light at the Devil's Elbow, a sharp bend in the road on a geological fault line in the rocks, where the road from Glossop enters the Longdendale Valley, as the scene of lovers fleeing from the evil one. The sudden appearance of the light saved the lovers from the attentions of the Prince of Darkness, freezing him in his tracks and causing his elbow to turn to stone, where it can still be seen on the skyline above the road. The lovers mysteriously disappeared and were said to have been spirited away to live with 'the fairies' but can occasionally be seen in the springtime sailing along, blown by the wind on the nearby reservoir as a pair of mute swans.

The Roman track at Doctor's Gate features in his tale of a learned doctor – a bit of a wizard like Faust who tricked the evil one in a race. The Devil hereabouts must be a bit slow, or the people of this area incredibly quick, and as we shall see, evidence inclines to the latter view. The doctor sold his soul for earthly fortune but when the time for payment came up he proposed a horse race to win it back as the poem tells.

Long years ago, so runs the tale

A doctor dwelt in Longdendale

Well versed in mystic lore was he

A conjuror of high degree

He read the stars that deck the sky

And told the rede of mystery

After giving him a head start the sporting Devil was just catching up and sadistically twisting the tail of the Doctor's steed from behind, while laughing hideously, when the poor beast sprang forward, losing its tail in the Devil's claws, and splashed through a stream. Running water is proof against witches, ghosts, ghouls and devils and the doctor was borne to safety on the other side as he had intended all along.

The Devil in a huff declared that the mortals of Longdendale would have no place to go when they died – as they were too bad for Heaven and too clever for Hell! The doctor was a real historical figure, Dr John Talbot, who became vicar of Glossop in 1496 and paid for the paving of the pack horse track now known as Doctor's Gate where it crosses Shelf Moor.

It has frequently been stated that a group of local families resident in and around the Longdendale Valley for countless generations are descendants of the original settlers from time beyond memory. A woman claiming to be a practitioner of earth magic claimed in radio and TV programmes that "Guardians of the Old Ways" still existed and looked after sacred wells and other sites associated with the Old Religion in the area. She appeared on documentary TV programmes broadcast in the 1970s and 80s.

David Kelsall's depiction of the carved faces on a stone found near the Etherow Valley

Since then little more has been heard. Have her descendants been seduced by Snapchat and its instant gratifications to the detriment of the Old Ways? Have the old wells grown mossy, choked and neglected now the Lights are no longer seen, unless as a chain of smartphones glowing in the dark?

New Age or modern day Celtophiles love to claim anything old and other worldly for rather 'pagan' ideals of a peaceful past when people were naturally wiser, gentler and incredibly in-tune with the land. But, curiously, recent ancestral DNA research has tended to support the notion that an unusual strain of ancient genes has passed down through the generations in this part of the Pennines. It was found that the grouping, which is concentrated just a bit further north centring around the old borders of West Yorkshire, may be a vestige of the Celtic Kingdom of Elmet.

Etymologists have pointed out that a high concentration of placenames with 'Celtic' derivations exist in Longdendale.

Tintwistle means 'a sprinkling.' Coombs Rocks, Beacom Houses and Compstall contain the celtic 'Cwm' for a valley. The name of the River Etherow is Celtic, as is Werneth, meaning place of alder trees. Glossop itself may derive from Celtic 'Glo' for sun (or coal). The sop is self explanatory. But spoilsports claim it is a shortform of the Saxon 'hope' for valley.

Elmet existed well into Anglo Saxon times and seems to have represented a sovereign Celtic state, able to govern itself and maintain a distinctive culture, isolated by bog and forest between the Northumbrian Angles to the north and the Mercian Angles to the south. A historian unkindly suggested that this was because their land was scrubby wet moor and not very attractive to the newcomers for would-be annexation! So they left their petty kingdom in peace.

The surreal League of Gentlemen comedy series was centred on and filmed in the village of Hadfield with their iconic 'Local Shop,' looming on the edge of Longdendale *"This is a local shop for local people, there's nothing for you here!"* outsiders were informed.

Groups of incomers to these islands (and to Glossop) arrived with the first nomads towards the end of the last ice age some 11,500 years ago – at which time they walked across from the continent following reindeer herds, the North Sea then being a flat plain intersected by rivers,(all the seawater was locked up in glaciers further north).

Prehistoric deer hunters

A Shaman finds magic mushrooms in the woods

It is said that pregnant reindeer cows seek high rocky barren areas away from predators to calve in the spring, and the Pennines may have provided such a refuge. Ancient bones and artefacts from Peak caves now in local museums provide evidence for the existence of both reindeer and humans who used flint tools to butcher them in the area.

Maybe it is coincidence that the coat of arms of the Borough of High Peak incorporates two stags – (or reindeer-like animals?), which may even have been the totem animal of the first comers to the area? It is well known that stag or reindeer horns form a totem headdress of shamans in their ritual dances, when with the assistance of herbal potions they assume the spirit of the animal and travel to an otherworld accompanied by ritual drumming, singing and dancing.

The Abbots Bromley horn dance, England's oldest dance tradition still incorporates thousand years old reindeer horns normally kept in the church as part of the dancer's ritual. The 'Celtic' Gundestrup silver cauldron found in a bog in Jutland shows a man sitting or dancing cross-legged wearing reindeer horns on his head, with a snake in one hand and a precious torc (neck ring) in the other.

Our own Christmas festivities involving Santa Claus and reindeer are thought to be a thinly disguised throwback to a winter fire festival involving eating or drinking delicacies made from the red and white spotted mushroom said to induce hallucinations of flying.

Chapter Two

Ritual stones amid the ruins

Nothing quite so grand as a silver cauldron has turned up yet in Longdendale, but some things of rather curious provenance have. The main focus of mystic interest is a round hill which dominates Glossop and Longdendale called Mouselow, known locally as Castle Hill. Scarred by old quarry workings, planted with trees and overgrown by scrub it also sports a hideous telecommunications tower at one end which does nothing for its venerable character, though keeping smartphone users in touch.

Some very strange objects have been discovered there, curious incidents occurred during an archaeological dig and evidence of alignments may prove it to be on a significant ley line.

In the mid 1700s there were still the remains of a stone castle with ditches and earthworks on the hilltop. It is said a small Catholic chapel was intended to have been erected here in 1780 but workmen digging foundations stopped when they broke into a vault and found 'summat odd'. It was near here in 1840 that retired Wesleyan minister, George Marsden, discovered some strangely carved stones.

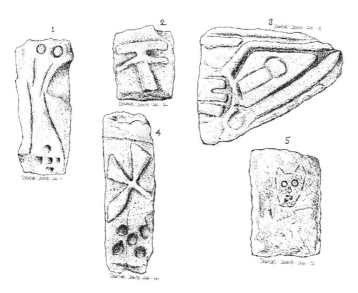

Marsden thought them curious enough to collect and incorporate in the eaves of his house in Hadfield (later the Spinners Arms).

There they remained exposed to the weather until requested by the Duke of Norfolk, the local landowner. He in turn eventually donated them to the newly formed Glossop Antiquarian Society who kept them in storage for fifty years.

A report of 1908 described them as probably of Anglo-Saxon workmanship and depicting among other things "Thoth, one of their gods". Now Thoth is an ancient Egyptian deity, nothing to do with the Anglo Saxons. But there are said to be other stone carvings, like the Egyptian ankh, the cross of life and symbol of the sun god, elsewhere in the Glossop area – according to the archaeologist who conducted a dig at Mouselow in 1984-86, Glynis Reeve.

Glynis had been tasked with surveying and re-excavating a trench dug by pupils from Glossop Grammar School under the supervision of a master, Mr J Scott, in 1963-64. She had the help of the University of Manchester archaeology unit and site assistants funded on a Manpower Services Commission project. Glynis conducted a careful dig and extended the trench.

It established that the castle was a rare Norman ringwork, likely based on a much earlier Iron Age hillfort. It had ditches and counterscarps and once possessed an outer bailey, although this had been much eroded by subsequent quarrying. Remains of stone buildings and a spiral stair were uncovered. A worked flint probably of prehistoric date was found deep in a tree root. There was a silted up spring decorated with quartz pebbles and a Bronze Age burial mound was found to have been disturbed by the ditches.

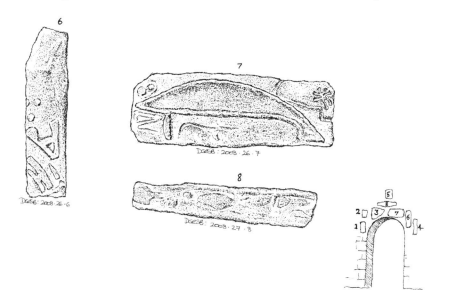

To complement the dig Glynis set up a small exhibition in a field centre based in Glossop where the public were invited to view details of the excavations. To make it more interesting the Mouselow carved stones were put on display as an example of what had been found there in the past.

Already, anxious local people had been turning up on site asking who the excavators were and what they were doing. Glynis assumed an exhibition would diffuse suspicion and create positive interest. One man came and stared at the stones for a long time then left, shaking from head to foot, saying they were evil and should be covered up. When Glynis commented that she wondered what it was people expected them to find another visitor turned and said,"The entrance to Hell!" She also received late night telephone calls warning of horned figures, the 'Old Ways', and even threatening that someone might end up nailed to a tree!

To allay tensions Glynis and two brave colleagues decided to visit the dig on the night of the Celtic festival of Beltane, in May. They were frightened by rustling in the trees and saw torches among the woods but Glynis stood in the middle of their excavations and said in a clear voice,"You have nothing to fear from us!" After that things seemed to calm down, the phone calls stopped and no-one else came into the field centre to complain.

The dig continued, concentrating on the archaeology, but Glynis decided that perhaps Mouselow was a site sacred to a tradition which was still using it for religious purposes. She had seen a Chronicle TV interview with a woman, whose identity was concealed, claiming to be a Guardian of the Old Ways in 1977.

Mouselow stones above a doorway in Buxton Museum before the gallery was changed

The same Guardian was re-interviewed for a new documentary screened in 1986 which also filmed the dig. The Guardian, declared it had brought "the wrong sort of publicity,"which had upset members of the old tradition. As to the stones themselves they were examined by two Celtic scholars, Professor Rosemary Cramp and Dr Anne Ross who both declared that their style suggested a Celtic Iron Age cultural tradition and may have once formed part of a shrine. There was an oral tradition of a Celtic burial ground near Hadfield and the eastern face of Mouselow has a number of flattened circles possibly of old burial mounds or hut circles.

It is impossible to say what the symbols on the stones represent. One looks like a phallus, others are like leaves or anvils. One seems to be a letter 'A' or cruck frame, another is like the face of a cat, or a horned animal, another could be a fish and one is said to be a woman with her hair in a bun, but special lighting is needed to see it. Two have five indentations like dominoes, known locally as the "valley pattern" to signify a woman. This female symbol is also recognised in geomancy or earth divination. The Celts of course worshipped a mother goddess.

The Mouselow stones ended up at Buxton Museum where they were assembled into an arch above a doorway in the Romano-British section of the old Museum layout. But while in storage at Glossop they are said to have been the cause of malfunctioning computers, and even a power failure, as if imbued with a magnetic field!

Nebra sky disk perhaps 3,600 years old found in Germany

In the latest new exhibition gallery at Buxton just one of the stones is on display but a pamphlet about them by Glynis is on sale.

Stranger still is the alleged existence of a copper disk supposedly found at Mouselow in 1962 by workmen clearing topsoil at an adjacent quarry. The disk bore an uncanny likeness to the celebrated Nebra sky disk, a unique Bronze Age artefact unearthed by metal detectorists in 1999 on a hill in Germany. The Nebra disk is made from bronze with a beautiful blue green patina from long contact with the damp earth, but its surface is decorated with celestial symbols in gold.

The Nebra disk is thought to have helped Bronze Age farmers 3,600 years ago with seasonal planting and harvesting, using astronomical observations, and shows the crescent moon, a sun or full moon, stars and the Pleiades star group. There are also gold strips on the rim representing the horizon and an enigmatic sun boat. It was first exhibited in 2004 although publicity about it surfaced when state police arrested the unlicensed detectorists and seized the disk from people they sold it to in 2002.

A UK website showing a copper disk with apparently similar gold moon sun and star symbols appeared about 2004 with two pages devoted to a description of the Mouselow sky disk and another page which seems to have been merely lifted from a scholarly description of the nearby Melandra Roman fort by the local heritage society.

The Mouselow disk pages contained a crude drawing on cheap lined paper of a supposedly collapsed stone altar under which workmen were said to have found the disk in 1962 and a photo of the disk itself, which had it been buried for any length of time would have been covered in green oxidisation, but showed only a small patch possibly induced by a weak acid like urine. From the photo the metal seems to have been cut by hand with a pair of metal shears and the 'gold' moon sun and stars may have been of base alloy like brass.

Neither Buxton nor Manchester museums know anything of the Mouselow disk's existence.

The suggestion that it was once exhibited at Glossop Heritage Centre is flatly denied by the heritage society who ran it and they are a bit tired of people who have seen the disk online asking them about it. Why should anyone have gone to the trouble of creating it as a hoax?

The publicity surrounding the Nebra disk at the time was possibly responsible, but also the fact that the Nebra disk sold for nearly one million deutschmarks on the black market before being retrieved may be another. The website's assertion that the gold on the Mouselow disk (which should have been treasure trove) was assayed by a bullion company in Birmingham who discovered it came from the Ashanti mines via Carthage, probably brought by Roman soldiers, is obvious nonsense.

The Mouselow disk is described as 5 inches in diameter, half the size of the Nebra disk. It is made of sheet copper, bronze would perhaps have been harder to obtain. The star group depicted is the Plough with the pole star above, the crescent moon and sun are similar to the Nebra disk but the solar boat has rowlocks instead of striated lines.

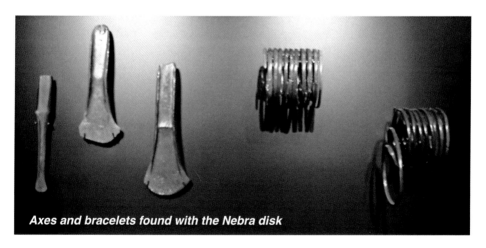

Axes and bracelets found with the Nebra disk

The Nebra disk was found buried in a pit inside the Mittelberg, a hilltop prehistoric enclosure deep in the Ziegetroda Forest in Saxony, an area containing a thousand burial mounds. It was buried within a hoard containing two bronze swords, two bronze axes a chisel and sections of a spiral bronze bracelet. All the finds are exhibited in a museum at Halle in Saxony. No other objects are said to have been found with the Mouselow disk and no- one knows where it is – but if anyone has any provenance, please share it with us? The Mouselow disk is exhibited in no museum and has so far been seen by no expert. This is fairly conclusive.

Mold gold cape British Museum

A number of prehistoric gold objects really have been discovered in northern Britain. One of the most interesting is the Mold cape, found in a burial mound in North Wales, associated with the story of a ghostly golden figure long before it was excavated by workmen building a road. It was probably a ritual garment and had been lying there undisturbed for about 3,600 years! Buxton Museum recently staged a temporary exhibition of golden torcs or neck rings found all over Britain. They also exhibit prehistoric gold coins from a cave found recently in Dovedale and other gold jewellery and coins have been recovered from Peak caves over the years.

Gold working was a Bronze Age technique and much of the native gold used came from Wales, Ireland and Cornwall. A small amount is known to have existed in the Derbyshire Peak, but there was more silver to be extracted from the abundant lead ore of the district.

Coin hoard from Dovedale

The oldest lead silver mine was close by Mam Tor, an outrigger of the Kinder plateau – an impressive Bronnze Age hillfort later belonging to powerful Celtic tribes who inhabited an area known as Brigantia. Mam Tor is Celtic for Mother Mountain and recalls the ancient worship of a threefold mother goddess – virgin, matron and hag. Dr Anne Ross was told by the Longdendale "Guardian" that some people of the valley on remote farms still acknowledge the triple Celtic mother goddess, decorate their wells and springs with garlands and light bonfires at Beltane on May 1 to ensure a good year. In Celtic areas a bannock cake was baked and the person who got the burnt bit was 'chosen' (i.e. would once have been sacrificed).

The many carved stone heads to be found locally in walls and houses, sometimes buried or beside wells she explained as part of an ancient belief that the spirit resides in the head and that a carved head was a talisman to ward off malevolent forces.

The Romans must have sensed these forces when they came to Longdendale in about 78 AD and built Melandra fort, known to them as Ardotalia 'the high dark valley'. During excavations in the 1960s within the levelled ruins of the abandoned fort evidence was discovered of legionary shrines lining a strongroom at the centre of the barrack blocks which housed the cohort of 500 men. Some of the Roman altars can be viewed in the new gallery at Buxton museum.

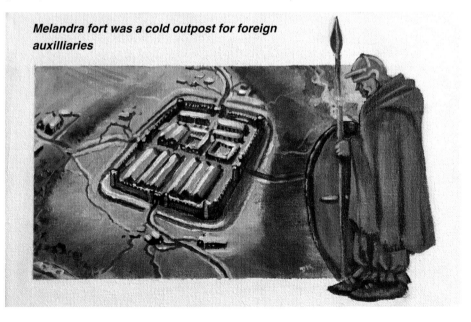

Melandra fort was a cold outpost for foreign auxilliaries

The fort lay at the junction of present day Glossop Brook and the River Etherow where it descends from the Longdendale Valley just below Hollingworth. It is situated about a mile beneath Mouselow hilltop which may also have been used by the Romans as a lookout or signal station. Nowadays the site of Melandra is hemmed in by Gamesley council estate, an industrial park and sewage works. But this cheerless spot may once have been of great significance.

It was a staging post between the major Roman fort and settlement at Manchester and the fort at Brough or Navio in the Hope Valley (close by Mam Tor in an area rich in metal ores).

First built in timber surrounded by triple ditches it was rebuilt in stone about 108 AD by two auxillary units of infantry soldiers – the 1st Cohort Frisiavones and the 3rd Cohort Bracara Augustani. These soldiers were recruited respectively from Frisian Germany north of the Rhine and Braca in Portugal.

The stone was quarried from Hargate Hill, where a Roman coin hoard has been found. They constructed stone walls backed by earthen ramparts and surmounted by corner watchtowers, and the four gates into the fort had twin towers on each. There was a bathhouse just outside the fort heated by a furnace, with a mansio for distinguished visitors and imperial messengers to stay nearby. A substantial vicus or civilian settlement existed under the present Gamesley council estate. Farmsteads close by may have been allotments to retired soldiers who had completed their 25 years' service. Some local families may be their descendants.

In 1771 antiquarian rector, the Rev John Watson recorded substantial above ground remains of the stone fort, including part of the bathhouse then in process of demolition. He seems to have coined the name Melandra signifying valley of oaks – the area once having been thickly forested. Watson also recorded the discovery of a memorial stone to Frisian centurion Valerius Vitalis now in Buxton museum.

The earliest written reference to the fort was by an unknown 7th century cleric in a manuscript which named it as Zerdotalia.

A dig in the late Victorian period revealed a spread of coins dating from one of Galba 69 AD to one of Magnus Maximus 383-388 AD, but the fort is thought to have been used mainly in the period 80 AD onwards for about 90 years. After abandonment it was fired and became a source of building stone with many pieces of masonry robbed and incorporated in later walls, bridges and houses. A large amount of surviving stones from Ardotalia Roman fort were reused in the building of medieval Mottram church.

Glass from window panes was recovered along with glass beads and the typical terracotta red earthenware tiles of roofs, walls and flooring in large quantities. These tiles may have been manufactured on site and bear the imprints of animal paws and human hands impressed while the clay was still wet. The author once found a nice red piece with a very clear human thumbprint in which the striated lines of a long dead tiler's hand were perfectly visible after 1,900 years!

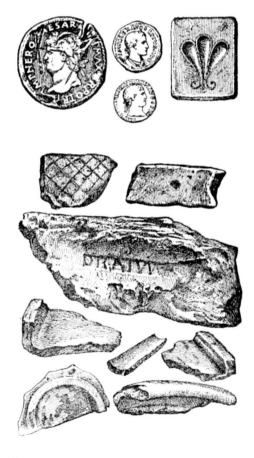

The routes of the roads to and from the fort were clearly recognisable and used until the 18th century when the era of toll road building took off and they became obliterated. There were many subsidiary local routes meandering to farms and settlements now visible only as crop marks in fields or farm tracks. But it is believed that an important Roman lateral route eventually linking the main north south Roman roads came through the district.

An iron spearhead found near Mouselow

Historians have regarded Doctor's Gate over the Snake Pass as one of these. At Devil's Dyke on Shelf Moor a subsidiary packhorse route, now part of the Pennine Way, cuts across Doctor's Gate and heads for Torside Clough, passing close by the strange hump known as Torside Castle. This has long been associated with tales of ghostly marching Roman soldiers. In such a remotely inhospitable spot it is highly unlikely a permanent camp was ever made and current thought is that it may be a natural eminence.

But it may have been a place where young legionaries were route marched to practice their exercises of digging and making a marching camp after slogging uphill in full kit from Melandra. The Bracara in their native Portugal were skilled hillfort builders and there are similar military practice features in an upland area near the Roman fort at Tomen y Mur in Snowdonia where other Roman units exercised. It would not have been a popular destination for them and they may have sometimes been obliged to do it on dark night exercises, doubtless carrying torches to illuminate the hazardous pitfalls all around. The chains of lights seen on these heights from Longdendale have sometimes been attributed to this legendary source, but the fact remains that no known Roman road ever crossed the hills at this point and Torside Castle itself has never been excavated to determine if it holds any archaeological clues.

Moorland looking towards Torside Castle

No-one knows exactly how Roman surveyors laid out their road plans*, but it is an interesting coincidence that a straight line drawn on a modern Ordnance Survey map links Melandra Roman fort with Mouselow Castle, a mile away on its hilltop and continued over the moors the line exactly crosses Torside Castle, though this is invisible from Mouselow.

Night exercise for the Roman Army at Torside Castle

Ley line enthusiasts will be excited to know that continuing eastwards the line cuts across various curious rock formations then reaches the start of the notoriously haunted Stocksbridge bypass. Westwards it crosses the ridge dominated by Mottram Church and runs straight towards the 'most haunted' area of Godley Green, described by Tom Middleton in his Legends of Longdendale over a hundred years ago – when these stories were already old.

The Romans' basic road surveying tool was the decempeda a ten foot rod, but this was supplemented with a whole array of other devices of increasing sophistication borrowed and refined from the Greeks, Egyptians and others, including alignments on the stars to ensure the accuracy of their straight lines.

Chapter Three

Lights and Leys

He was editor of the Ley Hunter magazine and author of many earth mysteries titles, yet Paul Devereux, once declared in an interview, "Ley lines don't exist, they just aren't there!"

Paul came to this startling conclusion after many years as director of the Dragon Project – an attempt to rationalise and collect objective evidence for geomantic ley line effects intersecting stone circles, burial chambers and other prehistoric features of the landscape. "There was some correlation with dowsing, but that is a subject open to speculation," he admits. "I don't doubt that some people have the ability to find underground water or buried metal using the rods, but ley lines are another matter."

Enthusiasts believe that leys are lines of vital energy joining significant points in the landscape and can be traced on a map using a ruler to join three or more features. They were first described by a Herefordshire antiquarian and landscape photographer Alfred Watkins in his book The Old Straight Track. "Imagine a fairy chain stretched from mountain peak to mountain peak as far as the eye could reach," he enthused. "Imagine mounds and standing stones acting as sight lines!" His own idea was that prehistoric people used them as a means of finding their way over trackless country.

Since the 1960s this theory was developed by devotees into ley lines being transmitters of a mystical earth energy or even ground beacon pathways to guide UFOs. There is some circumstantial evidence to suggest a high incidence of strange phenomena in the vicinity of known leys, particularly where they cross unusual ancient features, (such as Mouselow hillfort and Torside castle).

Longdendale in particular and the Peak in general record many sightings of mysterious lights, phantom aircraft and apparitions – to add to actual real lights, crashed aircraft and dead people scattered about the boglands.

Ley hunter Paul Devereux proposes an interesting theory about lightform phenomena or earth lights, an idea enthusiastically taken up by other investigators which has been applied to the Longdendale lights. Paul's idea is that the lights are a natural manifestation of earth energy generated by geological conditions existing in the Longdendale valley and elsewhere. The high rocky edges and deep ravines which shadow the southern face of the valley are criss crossed by large numbers of fault lines. In one ravine near Shining Clough a waterfall drops vertically down a significant fracture in the rock and this is the area where many of the light manifestations are said to occur.

Longdendale in the style of L S Lowry
private collection Cass Patton photo by Martin Greally

One of the more impressive witnesses of the phenomena is Sean Wood who lived at Bleak House on the north side of the valley just below the equally bleak and redundant Woodhead Chapel, (founded as a chapel of ease for weary travellers on this lonely route by a local lad made good and former Lord Mayor of London, Edmund Shaa, in 1487).

Sean's first experience of the lights was in the 1980s soon after moving into the house, when he thought someone was shining a bright light into his front room one night. Instead he realised the source was "a large pulsating ball of light" hovering above Shining Clough on the opposite side of the valley and across the reservoir. Puzzled and concerned he phoned the warden at Crowden youth hostel nearby to be told they could see it too. Yet there were no roads or even paths up Shining Clough in those days, however there is now a shooters' track onto the grouse moors.

Since then he reckons he must have seen the lights about 30 times – either as a large pulsating light on its own moving back and forth, or as a string of lights moving in an arc high on the hillsides. "There are bright lights which appear at the top end of Longdendale, there's no doubt they exist, but I've no idea what they are,"he concludes.

Many times the mountain rescue team has been alerted from Crowden or Glossop to investigate sightings. A Glossop Mountain Rescue Team member reported in 1978 that there had been frequent calls about lights: "Sometimes looking like a string of walkers carrying torches, that drifted about and then faded away. Other times it's been like a searchlight coming out of the hillside."

A trainee teacher, Mrs Barbara Drabble, wife of a National Park warden at Tintwistle gave a very clear account of her sighting in the summer of 1970. "It was past midnight but still quite warm and I was driving along admiring the view, thinking this must be the most beautiful place in the world to live, when suddenly from somewhere on Bleaklow there shone the most brilliant blue light. It lit up the bottom half of Bleaklow, all the railway, the reservoirs and a two mile stretch of the road. As I drove into it the car went icy cold and I quickly put the window up. The air appeared to vibrate. The light had the same piercing brightness as lightning but this light lasted some three or four minutes. It then disappeared as suddenly as it had come. I was terrified."

Strangely no-one else had seen the light and even seemed reluctant to discuss it. However the following summer in July a similar brilliant bluish light appeared on Bleaklow, illuminating the hostel at Crowden and was seen by all the residents. This time locals admitted seeing it and also having seen the lights before. Mrs Drabble's husband Ken led a search party up Torside Clough to try to locate the source, their large search and rescue lamp 'with a lens like a dustbin lid' was a tiny pinprick of light when viewed from the hostel and naturally nothing was found, getting all the gear up there would have taken the best part of an hour at least.

Shining Clough with mist devils

Flare type lights have often been reported over the moors. I saw a red one at about 8am one clear sunny morning rising above the moors near Uppermill and Greenfield in 1975, which was featured in the Huddersfield Daily Examiner. Normally flares are associated with distress calls possibly from injured walkers and climbers. Policemen and motorists frequently saw strange lights and flares over the moors between Oldham and Huddersfield in the 1970s. But search parties rarely found the cause. A pub at Standedge on the highest point of the road as it crosses into West Yorkshire was even called the Floating Light.

To give just one example from Longdendale a green flare was reported rising over Torside Clough in February 1982 by a resident of Torside Cottages, but a search by Glossop MRT found nothing. A mountain rescue team member said:"If it happened once it would be put down to the work of a prankster, but when it happens year after year this becomes unlikely. It happens too often to be just chance." However there is a suggestion that some of the flares were home made and fired from locations in Glossop and that spent cases had been found.

Longdendale cuts a deep slice into the southern Pennine chain, of a wild beauty which appeals to all who love dramatic rocky edges overhanging the rough pasture, conifer plantations, and a string of large reservoirs. It also carries a main trunk road with continual sounds of heavy trucks, high tension power lines slung between giant steel pylons, and a formerly electrified railway which once linked Manchester and Sheffield, now a cycleway and walkers route, the Longdendale Trail.

It has none of the sylvan beauty of the Woodlands Valley a few miles south, or the Holme Valley a few miles north, and is surrounded by the frowning moors of Bleaklow and Black Hill (once described by a visitor as, "a prodigious muck heap") and said to be one of the most forbidding spots in the Peak, where the first army ordnance surveyors couldn't find a dry level spot to plant their theodolites. Now it has stone flagged pathways over the peat bogs to the trig point.

Shining Clough across the reservoir

Naturally it is a place for dramatic happenings – as a small boy in the 1960s I witnessed a violent thunder and lightning storm crackling across Longdendale above the conifers, the craggy rocks, and the reservoirs opposite to Bleak House. No wonder strange electrical phenomena could manifest here. In those days the only electrified rail line across the Peak came down the valley. High tension cables hummed with thousands of volts carrying power for the national grid and large bodies of electrically conductive water heaved restlessly in the valley bottom, above a large fault line from Shining Clough which runs diagonally across in the direction of Bleak House and Crowden.

Woodhead tunnel entrances, now used for high tension power cables

Just up the valley the longest rock bored twin railway tunnels, driven under the moors in the 1840s cost the lives of scores of tough navvies in accidents and when the track was closed and taken up in the 1980s, the CEGB fed their high tension cables into them. Differences in atmospheric pressure on either side of the hills means that terrific winds are sometimes generated at the tunnel mouth.

Paul Devereux writes: "Earth lights may be related to ball lightning and earthquake lights, both of which are recorded but unexplained. They are terrain related and in some places locals have seen them for generations." He believes pressures in the earth's crust could cause electro magnetic fields to give birth to the lights. "There are eyewitness reports of columns of light emerging from the ground and lightballs forming within or at their upper ends. These globes of light can flash off over surrounding countryside.

"On occasion a sphere of light is seen hovering above the ground perhaps attached to the earth by a strand of energy, these types of light just spring into visibility. People who see the lights close-to report a teeming, wriggling light effect within the outline of the lightform."

Paul believes the effect is rather like electrical plasma, a glowing mass of light-emitting photons. Curiously, blobs of plasma generated in laboratory conditions start to behave like organisms – as if possessed of a rudimentary sentience.

We do not know if anyone has seen the Longdendale lights that close up, although it is a widespread belief in folklore that to get so close to such a light can be fatal. The rocky moorland edges on the southern side of the valley, where the lights are mainly seen, are intersected by tumbling streams, particularly in the vicinity of Shining Clough (a suggestive name, with origins lost in the mists of time).

Something lighting up the moors at night? Longdendale lights

Old residents who farmed the valley pointed to Nell's Pike a rocky edge above the Devil's Elbow as a source of ghostly lights. But perhaps this was because they had heard Tom Middleton's story about the mystery light which froze the Devil's arm into a rock there, or maybe their grandparents had repeated that tale long before Middleton came and copied it down? A live webcam operated here for a number of years and attracted thousands of online visitors, but managed to record nothing of interest.

Someone who did get a close-up encounter there, but not with one of the Longdendale lights, was railwayman John Davies who lived in a cottage in the valley. He was long retired and in his eighties when he eventually shared this weird experience, which happened as he returned to Woodhead on his motorbike one moonlit night in the 1950s.

A slithery encounter near Devil's Elbow

"I was on my motorbike on a section of the road known as the Devil's Elbow. The moon lit everything up as bright as day and as I rounded the corner, level with the farm, something sort of told me to stop. A great black wall appeared in front. I couldn't see through it. I had to stop right in front of it. It didn't frighten me but I had a queer sensation. It was like a massive black slug sliding across t' road and up t' moor. It had a head just like a whale and a white eye with a black pupil going round and round. After it disappeared I got off and had a look, but there was nothing there."

Mr Davies described his encounter as between Ogden Clough and the track which enters the road above Higher Deepclough farm. He added: "I've been over there thousands of times but never seen anything like it. I've heard many stories about ghosts of Roman soldiers being seen on the moors. They are supposed to appear on the night of the first full moon in spring. I'd believe anything about this valley, it's a weird place at night."

The Manchester Evening News carried an article in 1979 about walkers on the Pennine Way, which passes close by Torside Castle, encountering, "two or three ghostly Roman soldiers wandering on Bleaklow". More details are lacking but the walkers reported it to National Park wardens who passed information to the mountain rescue team, (but they may have been a bit late to help?).

An earlier sighting on the Doctor's Gate track where it crosses Hope Woodlands occurred in 1932 when on a blustery night four climbers breathlessly arrived at Crookstone Barn in Edale and described how they had lain in the heather and watched, "a Roman legion march past in the lane," even describing the distinctive curved shields of the soldiers and their curiously shaped helmets.

All these sightings must be offset against the thousands of walkers and climbers who regularly traverse these boglands and see nothing which can't be explained. On some days the Pennine Way scar at Devil's Dyke is thronged with strollers in the sunshine – many will have parked their cars at nearby Snake Summit. They are walking within easy reach of several crashed aircraft, the vistas are magnificent, you can see for miles and the human traffic is as crowded as Oxford Street.

But on other days when the mists close in and shapes shift, or when the full moon's light beams on and off between scudding clouds, blown by a wind which howls and screams like the Devil, this is a place where anything could happen. And perhaps it does.

Chapter Four

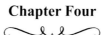

The Old Woman gathers them in

An area of Bleaklow has been associated by local people with an ancient spirit of the moors sometimes known as T'Owd Woman, or even Th'Owd man, seen occasionally as a suggestive yet shapeless form in the mist from time out of mind. The name 'Old Woman' appears on ordnance survey maps just off Devil's Dyke as it snakes towards Bleaklow Head.

In the spring lambing season when sudden snow showers can become terrific blizzards as late as March or April young farmers fretting about ewes still on the hillsides were reassured by the old people. "Don't worry. Biddy'll take care of her own." Meaning T'Owd Woman had an eye out, looking after her sheep and gathering in her lambs.

She seems to be a vestige of the old Celtic earth mother belief, an aspect of the threefold mother goddess once personified locally by Brigantia, in other regions known as Bride or Bridget associated with wells, flocks and fecundity and possibly in this instance huddled in the guise of old crone or hag, the watchful guardian of flocks. Various stones are known to have been carved with the triple faces of the goddess. It has even been said there is always a living 'Mother' in this part of Derbyshire – one who is mother to her people, a wise woman, an intermediary between them and mother earth who provides all.

The name 'Biddy' now a disreputable colloquialism for an old lady was used by the older folk with respect to T'Owd Woman and out of gratitude for her guardianship and care. It could be a dialect corruption or nickname for the goddess Brigantia. Celtic scholars believe her to have been the tutelary deity of the district and probably for the whole of the Pennines.

The peaks which rise up to crown these moors reach a deceptive ceiling at Bleaklow Head's 2,060ft while Higher Shelf Stones is just slightly lower at 2,039ft rivalling nearby Kinder Scout's slightly higher 2,088ft the loftiest point in the southern Pennines. No wonder then that the area is littered with the scattered wreckage of aircraft which tragically didn't make it over this often invisible rolling ridge of high ground and isolated rocky outcrops so frequently shrouded in low cloud or thick mist.

The remains of 50 aircraft whose histories are known, dating from a WW1 bi-plane which downed near Torside reservoir Longdendale in 1919 to a Bell helicopter which came to grief on Kinder in 1997, are located around the high moors. In most cases the 200 or so crew died on impact, just occasionally the lucky ones crawled from the wreckage. Of these, in the relatively small area around Bleaklow, no fewer than seven aircraft crashed in the years 1939-1948, at the cost of 34 lives most of them lost during WW2.

Perhaps the most tragic was the crash of giant USAF B-29 Superfortress "Over Exposed" a photo reconnaissance plane, which gained its name from photographing two atom bomb tests at Bikini Atoll in the Pacific a couple of years before. It had also recently taken part in the Berlin airlift and was due with its crew for a spot of home leave.

On Nov 3rd 1948 pilot Captain Landon Prentice Tanner took off from the former Dambusters base at RAF Scampton in Lincolnshire on a short routine hop over the Pennines to deliver a payroll and some mail to USAF staff at RAF Burtonwood near Warrington. With him was his crew of 10, and two passengers.

Cloud obscured the hills, and flying just too low to clear the 2,039ft rising ground at Higher Shelf Stones the giant silver aircraft ploughed into the peat hags and gravel, breaking up and bursting into flames. All thirteen on board were killed with bodies scattered across the moorland – where an RAF Mountain Rescue team found them just as light was fading in a steady drizzle, garishly illuminated by flames from burning debris reflected on the Superfortress' gigantic fully intact tailplane, towering over all like a beacon on top of the cold and misty moor.

In recent times the crash site has become a magnet for the curious, thanks to posts on social media. Extreme weather and souvenir hunters have taken their toll on the debris, but a fair amount still remains, looking rather like a scrapyard on the moors – the Wright Cyclone engines, bits of wing and fuselage, undercarriage and twisted aluminium. None should be removed, but one find had a rather curious outcome and perhaps souvenir hunters should take serious note!

'Overexposed' flying too low over the misty moors

In case anyone thinks the payroll is still up there, the story is that USAF military police arrived pronto after the crash and recovered $7,400 in a locked fireproof satchel although that doesn't sound a lot for a base which, during the war, accommodated up to 18,000 service personnel.

However in the 1970s an aviation historian from nearby Hadfield, Gerald Scarratt, found another treasure. While picking through the clinging peat around the wreck after heavy rain he spotted what looked like a brass washer. On removing the soil he discovered a gold wedding ring and on the inside was inscribed the owner's name – Landon P. Tanner, the pilot of the ill fated Superfortress.

Shortly after this discovery the historian took up a group of aircraft enthusiasts who wished to see the site. "I bent down to show them where I found the ring and when I looked up they had scarpered and were 10 or 15 yards away. When I caught up with them they were ashen faced. They said they had seen someone standing behind me looking down and dressed in full flying uniform."

After this the group decided they had seen enough and headed back for the road. Gerry had seen nothing and was eventually able to trace Capt. Tanner's daughter, Jean, and reunite her with her father's ring. She and her husband made a special pilgrimage to pay their respects at the tragic site. It is worth noting that all the bodies were recovered after the crash and stretchered off the moors. Capt. Tanner now rests in a military cemetery in the U.S.

Other people have had strange impressions on this spot. A BBC TV producer who wanted to do a film there told the Peak National Park officer who took her up that she had to get back to her car because, "I just feel uncomfortable here."

There is a feeling that things deposited on the moor somehow become a part of the place, almost like a votive offering to the local earth spirit, so that if anything is removed the atmosphere is disturbed and can wreak revenge if compensation is not made.

A number of curious incidents support this idea. Ron Collier an aviation historian researched many tales of aircraft on the moors. One was of a farmer who took some useful bits of fuselage from the wreck site of a Bristol Blenheim which crashed on Sykes Moor above Longdendale in 1939. He stored them in a barn but soon after he and his son were shocked to witness the building nearly shake itself to pieces. Convinced it was to do with the wreckage he quickly returned it to the moor and the phenomena ceased, never to recur.

Ron unfortunately gave a propeller from the same site to a friend. When they met up a year later the friend was a changed man. In twelve months his business had collapsed, his wife left him and his children had also gone. "You gave me that propeller," he accused Ron. Needless to say it was returned to the moor.

John Davies the railwayman who lived in Longdendale also took some perspex from the crash site and stored it in his garage. He and a friend one night soon after heard, "a very large animal sniffing around outside." It was an uncanny feeling and John's father suggested, "if I was you I'd take that back where you got it from." He reburied it on the moor.

The crash of the Blenheim was no more tragic than any of the others, but there is some evidence that the two young pilots may have tried to parachute before the plane struck as their bodies were found back along the flightpath, which suggests the plane must have already been in trouble before it crashed.

Ron Collier said: "There is a force which governs the moors. You can feel it. Scores of sightings only backs that up. Something is going on and it is very difficult to explain what." Although he sought a logical explanation Ron felt the incidents were more akin to the paranormal.

In the years 1939-48 as many as seven aircraft crashed around Bleaklow with 34 crew and passengers killed. The Blenheim was the first, followed in August 1941 by a Boulton Paul Defiant night fighter and in December of that year with a Blackburn Botha bomber. In only one crash were there survivors. Two crewmen, a navigator and a gunner were saved from the wreck of a Wellington bomber in January 1943, though the three others died. The crash of a Lancaster bomber nearby in May 1945 cost the lives of all six crew, and a Dakota troop carrier came down soon after, killing another seven men.

Last flying Lancaster at Ladybower – photo Anthony Boardman

Not surprisingly people still report seeing what they imagine to be large WW2 propeller driven aircraft silently flying low along the valleys and over the moors, swerving into ridges and disappearing from sight. On occasion this has led to full scale searches by rescue services without anything being found.

It is well known that the famous wartime Dambuster squadron practised bombing runs over the Derwent and Howden dams on the edge of the moors leading to Bleaklow. A flypast has become a regular commemorative event for the RAF's remaining flying Lancaster bomber to entertain summer crowds over the Derwent Dam, the west tower of which contains a memorial to members of 617 Squadron RAF who flew and died in the raid over Germany in WW2.

So occasionally a real WW2 aircraft in camouflage colours is seen flying low along the Peak valleys. In addition, large NATO Hercules aircraft, with four wing-mounted turbo propeller driven engines and drab grey-green camouflage, glide silently down the valleys, practising their low level flying skills, looking remarkably like WW2 planes. This vision has surprised many a walker and motorist – a sudden quiet appearance seemingly at treetop height, and instantaneous disappearance behind a neighbouring ridge, with the engine roar following a moment later – interpreted by some as an impact explosion.

I have seen them myself close up and can testify to the sense of drama, but as a former reporter at air shows and ex-defence ministry information officer I know what they are.

Perhaps we can conclude this chapter with the story of two schoolboys who in about 1960 climbed one clear and frosty morning onto the moors near Higher Shelf Stones with the excited intention of collecting souvenirs from the Superfortress crash site. After a picnic on a wheel of the scattered aircraft debris they wandered the peat groughs, eyes to the ground looking for portable bits.

Wild moorland valley said to be sacred to Guardians of the 'Old Ways'

Suddenly one let out a yell: "Bloody hell, what is it?" His friend, who later became a seasoned member of Glossop Mountain Rescue Team takes up the story.

"He was pointing to the wild lonely swamp called Grains in the Water, at the head of Hern Clough. Suddenly I saw grouse exploding out of the heather towards us, sheep and hares stampeding towards us, and behind them, rolling at a rapid rate, a low bank of cloud or fog. And in it but leading it and striding purposefully forwards was a huge shadow figure, a man-like silhouette, but bigger than a man, as high as the cloudbank, as high as a house.

Something spooky came drifting out of Hern Clough 'as big as a house'

And the terror that hit me and was driving all the animals and my friend was utterly overwhelming – like a physical blow. I have never felt the like since!

"We fled. We plunged over the crags above Gathering Hill. We fled in mindless terror down that mountainside towards Doctor's Gate and Shelf Brook and all the sheep or wildlife that could run or fly went careering down with us in utter panic. And then about half way down we seemed to run out into sunlight – and it was all over. The sheep put their heads down and started to graze and everything returned to normal. But back up there, on Higher Shelf Stones, wisps of mist were still coiling round."

Having been back many times including search and rescue missions in the dark the man is still convinced that he had a brush with Th'Owd Lad on that sunlit moor.

"Don't ask me to rationalise it. I do think that every now and then some of us stumble into an encounter with elements deeper and older than we are, and they are not by their nature, benevolent, though they may be. This certainly wasn't."

Chapter Five

Grand Cross on the moors?

What about the other areas the mysterious ley line over Bleaklow reaches? It tracks off into the more populous areas of South Yorkshire to the east and Greater Manchester to the west.

In the east it links with an area well known for strange reports connected to (or sparked off by) the building of the Stocksbridge Bypass. There seems to have been some vestige of belief in hooded figures, possibly cowled monks, haunting this area from earlier times, but they got a boost in the 1980s when security men on the construction site, local police patrolmen, and eventually drivers on the completed bypass started to report fantastic sightings, as a larger than usual number of accidents began to occur.

Rationalists have put down the accidents to the fact that the bypass was originally conceived as a dual carriageway, but expense and the narrowness of the cutting through the rocky hillsides above Stocksbridge meant it became instead a narrow pair of single carriageways, where dangerous overtaking caused head on collisions. Some attempt at speed control has reduced this.

But the legends persist. Legend number one is the existence of a nearby Priory – no such place is historically known, although a number of local farms were owned by a distant abbey. Legend number two concerns children in old fashioned clothes said to have been seen by the security guards and others playing in a field near Hunshelf Bank. Explanations suggest they are ghostly victims of a mine accident, or a Victorian carriage turning over on a day out.

To back this up one motorist overtaking a horsedrawn carriage on the finished bypass claims he saw it disappear as he passed.

Other drivers have seen hooded figures near Pearoyd Bridge and one psychic medium from Penistone claimed a dark shape materialised inside her car, forcing her to recite the Lord's Prayer to get rid of it!

A hooded shape was seen near Pearoyd Bridge

The ley line from Glossop comes over the moors and crosses the area in the vicinity of Langsett and Midhopestones higher up the valley, but dowsers say that leys are merely a guidance system for lines of energy, which can be traced with their dowsing rods, spiralling around the ley for some distance and loosely attached. If a negative strand reached Hunshelf, it has made a negative vortex!

In September 1987 security guards Steven Brookes and David Goldthorpe were patrolling the unfinished bypass. They had previously spotted children in a nearby field singing and dancing around a pylon who disappeared before they reached them, leaving no prints in the muddy ground. One evening soon afterwards they encountered a figure standing on the newly built flyover known as Pearoyd Bridge.

Brookes stayed below watching the man as Goldthorpe drove his vehicle up to the bridge and directed his headlights onto the figure. They both saw a darkly cloaked shape, but the light seemed to pass straight through it, and to add alarm to injury it had no head! Within seconds it had disappeared. The shocked men reported to their supervisor and soon after sought the advice of a local priest, who asked the police to investigate the site.

Within days PC Dick Ellis and Special Constable John Beet visited the bypass in a patrol car at night. After sitting for a while in the warm evening chatting and admiring the full moon, PC Ellis put down the window, then spotted something in the rear view mirror. Simultaneously SC Beet let out a scream. He later described seeing the face of a man in Dickensian clothing staring at him very intensely for a split second, pressed up against his side window.

A series of loud bangs against the rear of the patrol car followed which rocked it with the impact, but though both jumped out and looked around nothing could account for it. Earlier they had seen what they thought was a suspicious shape near the foot of Pearoyd Bridge, but decided it was just a tarpaulin cover blowing in the wind. Now quite unnerved they headed for the police station at Deepcar where a most unusual police report was written up!

All these men stuck to their stories even though it did them no good in their responsible jobs. PC Ellis when interviewed for Strange but True said imagination was ruled out because they had both experienced the same thing. The security firm boss of Brookes and Goldthorpe said that both men became for a time unemployable.

One emigrated to Canada where he later received psychiatric therapy for post traumatic stress.

At the other end, towards Greater Manchester, the ley line crosses notoriously haunted Godley Green as it tracks towards the west. Tom Middleton mentions several well authenticated stories of this area in his Legends of Longdendale. He personally interviewed people who had experiences and was assured: "There are more boggarts in Godley Green than anywhere in the kingdom!"

This is still a comparatively rural area on the fringes of Hyde and Hattersley, (two towns associated with convicted mass murderers, Dr. Harold Shipman, Myra Hindley and Ian Brady). But most of the stories recounted by Middleton occurred in the 19th century long before they were born. Some of the old farmhouses mentioned in the stories are standing today.

One of the haunted farms on Godley Green

One of the more famous, which has found its way into countless books of ghost stories, is the tale of a farmhouse beset for years with a noisy poltergeist which would rattle pans, break pots, tumble fire irons, open and close doors, cause bedclothes to be wrenched back, shake beds and stomp up and down stairs.

Farm servants ran screaming from the house and at least one young man gave up on his sweetheart when he heard the noise made by their 'boggart' in the farm kitchen. A rocking chair once set in violent motion would only stop when the farmer's wife sat in it and held it fast. But the most quoted incident was after she was returning from Gee Cross one night with her mother on a balmy summer's evening when suddenly the thorn hedge beside them was violently shaken by a sudden gust and on the other side they both saw a white shape, possibly a light or the draped figure of a woman moving rapidly across the field away from the farmhouse. When they got home they discovered that the young farmer had just died.

Another old cottage on the other side of the Green above a steeply wooded valley where eerie coiling mists gather of an evening was haunted by the ghost of an old woman. "Nanny" was often seen outside in the garden or the lane and peered in through the windows at the occupants with her wizened face. All agreed that she was dressed in an old country fashion in a bonnet with her long skirts tucked up and a white apron in front which she would shake violently at anyone who saw her, uttering a hissing "ish,ish,ish!" sound, as if trying to scare away animals. Many people reported that detail.

Perhaps the strangest manifestation of the area is the ghost hound of Godley Green. This probably belongs to a very ancient tradition of haunting and one with its roots in prehistory. The ghostly hound was well known to local farmers and most saw or heard it at some time or other. It was described as of a tawny colour, like a lion, had an enormous slavering head and great yellow eyes, seemingly of the mastiff type and was known to chase cattle at night with a great baying voice.

It was associated with a ruined cottage by the wayside and an old well, where it could sometimes be seen peering into the water. Many people encountered it in the lanes and instantly recognised the beast's uncanny form. The best account was by a fishmonger who delivered fresh fish to the local farms and was interviewed personally by Middleton in 1906. "It was as big as a cow," he insisted, declaring he hoped never to see it again if he lived to be a hundred (cows were a bit smaller in those days).

"I suddenly saw the thing beside me. It kept pace with me. If I stopped it stopped, if I ran, it ran, I could not overtake it." In fear the fishmonger lashed out at the ghostly animal, but found that his knuckles passed straight through the spectre and grazed against the hedge beyond.

"My blood ran cold and I was terribly frightened. Then it ran in front of me, then it passed me and came back again. It did not turn round to do this but its head was in front as it returned. As soon as it had passed I took to my heels as fast as I could run and never looked back. It was the most hideous thing I ever saw. Its feet went pit-a-pat, pit-a-pat, with a horrible clanking noise."

When Middleton helpfully suggested it might have been a cow the fishmonger shook his head solemnly. "It was no cow, it was a ghost. I never want to see the thing again!"

Now an ambitious plan to build 2,500 houses on Godley Green is being urged by Tameside Council. One wonders what the future occupants will experience?

A lone walker traverses the Pennine Way at Torside Clough, an ancient track used from Roman times to prehistory

Torside Castle on Bleaklow seems to form the hub of the ley, and what is even more intriguing is that ley hunters have discovered another line which crosses it at this very point forming a grand cross on the moors. The second ley also links places connected with the Romans, although it is orienteered in another direction entirely – heading north west towards Castleshaw Roman camp above Oldham and south east towards Navio Roman fort in the Hope valley.

Travelling along Torside Clough over Bleaklow it is on a prehistoric trackway used by traders in stone axes almost before the dawn of time, according to A.E. and E.M.Dodd the celebrated authors of Peakland Roads and Trackways.

Early hunter gatherers had used locally available sharp flakes of dark chert found in limestone as tools and weapons in place of flint, which is more abundant in chalklands further south.

But by the time of the first farmers in the Neolithic, about 5,000 years ago, sturdy axes were needed for tree felling to make pasture for farm animals and fields for growing grain.

These were imported from a Stone Age axe "factory" at Great Langdale in the Lake District. Made from very hard igneous rock, polished examples found in the Derbyshire uplands can be seen in Buxton Museum, and were probably carried along this ancient route. "These trade routes would follow well drained ridges – they would be 'ridgeways' and would require very little constructional work except where they had to cross a valley," the Dodds asserted following extensive research on old roadways.

Prior to this period routeways would have been almost unknown, as nomadic hunters roamed across vast trackless areas, following migrating herds of game animals like reindeer, while living in tents made from skins, or flimsy shelters of branches and handy caves en route. Established tracks only later became a feature of a permanently settled way of life. To avoid becoming lost in thick forest and scrubland early pioneers would move from one identifiable high point or landscape feature to another.

Eventually over generations a roadway would be formed by constant usage. The imprint of many human feet, often probably naked of any footwear, would have left a lasting impression on the bare clay and soil of the ancient ridgeways. The more rocky ways trampled and worn by the hooves of their pack animals left their signature on the landscape.

The second ley line has been plotted heading NW from Hope Valley to the concrete trig point at Blackden Edge on Kinder, across the Woodlands Valley up Lady Clough, over Higher Shelf Stones where the Superfortress came down, on towards Torside Castle, over the earthwork at Torside Reservoir over Long Ridge Moss, past waterfalls above Ashway Gap, by Boggart Stones on the edge of Saddleworth Moor and on to Castleshaw fort above Diggle.

In Hope Valley can be seen the outline of the Roman fort at Navio near Brough, once garrisoned by Roman troops from Aquitaine and like Melandra, having a substantial vicus or civil settlement nearby. The fort was occupied from 75 AD for about 200 years in this important lead mining area, where silver was also known to be extracted from the lead ore. Coins and pottery have been found on the site together with a memorial commemorating a Prefect in the reign of Emperor Antoninus – Capitonius Fuscus who in 158 AD oversaw the rebuilding of the fort in stone.

Stone from Navio Roman Fort

A gritstone altar dedicated in honour of the local Goddess Arnemetia, (who presided at the sacred grove beside the warm springs in Buxton), was excavated at Navio by John Garstang in 1903 down a flight of steps in an underground stone walled chamber. Archaeological evidence from the 1960s suggested that the strongroom had been sacked, probably during a rebellion in 193 AD when the fort was trashed about 35 years after the rebuilding. Altar and memorial stone can be seen at Buxton Museum.

The fort at Castleshaw near Saddleworth was built in a similar period about 79 AD when Roman Governor Agricola was remorselessly pressing further northwards in his annexations of territory while Rome was still in its expansionist phase. Castleshaw, whose Roman name may have been Rigodunum, guarded a major east west lateral route between Manchester and York and despite being at a high elevation exposed to the weather, also acquired a civilian vicus just outside the gates of the fort, and had a stone bread oven for making wood fired pizzas, so the Romans didn't leave all the comforts of civilisation behind them!

It's perfectly conceivable that a NW/SE subsidiary route taking advantage of an existing prehistoric trackway could have been used by the Romans to enhance their carefully engineered network of roads in case of emergencies.

All that remains of the strongroom at Navio

These Viae Diverticulae would have been more than justified in a region which Pliny describes as abounding in lead and silver.

Another still extant vestige of ancient culture was manifested here as late as the 1980s when a stone gatepost on Castleshaw Moor was carved into the primeval shape of a half human, half animal deity with curled ram's horns, a man's face and women's breasts.

Unfortunately it was soon smashed in two and defaced, but whether by an angry landowner, capricious sculptor, or act of random vandalism we do not know.

Chapter Six

Crusading Knights and a lost treasure

Dark Kinder! Standing on thy whin-clad side, where storm and solitude and silence dwell, and stern sublimity hath set her throne – I look upon a region wild and wide: A realm of mountain, forest haunt and fell, and fertile valleys beautifully lone.

John Critchley Prince

The great bulk of Kinder Scout looms over the Peak District as a colossal black brooding ridge, when viewed from almost any angle below. It is the area's official 'mountain' reaching the dizzying height of 2088ft, somewhere in the midst of a seemingly endless patchwork of water channels cut 15-20ft deep into brown peat which crowns the plateau. Here and there in the wilderness are outcrops of wind sculptured rock cut into fantastic shapes, but the most dramatic features are lofty jagged gritstone edges rearing high above the sudden scarp slopes beneath.

Dark Kinder wild and wide

Kinder Downfall is the Scout's most famous feature and may have bestowed the plateau's name, from 'scut' a runnel, and Kinder the name of a local family. Here most of the waters collected on the plateau disgorge into a dramatic waterfall which runs wildly over naked bedrock, and between tumbled boulders leaping suddenly into space and the valley below. When the west wind blows strongly the waters are dashed back high into the air creating an effect like a gigantic spray of Prince of Wales feathers visible for miles against the black nick on the edge. Another name for the feature is "Old Woman Brewing."

Then as winter winds blow and Kinder is transformed into an arctic wilderness reminiscent of the last ice age, the cascades are frozen into a fantastic ice palace creating caves of gigantic icicles over the rocks.

Members of the Kyndwr Club at the frozen Downfall early 1900s

There was once a real cave made from a wrack of tumbled rocks, with a clear pool floored in golden sand. Here the legend of the mermaid was born – those who peered into the waters of the pool on Easter eve' and saw her silhouette could be granted immortality!

Sadly a tremendous winter storm in Victorian times carried the rocks, cave, and pool over the edge of the Downfall for ever. But the legend persisted and is now repeated about a poor peaty black pond surrounded by tussock grass a mile away in the valley.

It is difficult to imagine, when walking up here early enough on a clear day, breathing the air of freedom, which seems to blow directly from the sea, hearing the cry of the lonely curlew on the wind, that a matter of a few miles away mundane urban life, streets and cars and shops and suburban homes exist, utterly oblivious to the proximity of this sublime primeval grandeur.

As it once was, so it is now, when anyone may traverse the wilderness, but time was when permission was required. Most recently this was challenged by the Kinder Trespass in 1932 when walkers and gamekeepers clashed and several ramblers were sent to jail. But the right to roam and the establishment of the Pennine Way put paid to all that.

About two miles south along the edge from the Downfall is Kinder Low End and there, not far from an unexplored prehistoric burial mound is a hidden cavern entrance. Caves are not common in gritstone country and this one is probably the result of subsidence in the compact masses of gritstone perched on the edge sliding forward over softer shale, fracturing and forming cavities.

In 1843 The Manchester City News recorded an incident when two youths were trapped here after an adventure which went wrong. They both worked at Clough Mill in Little Hayfield and one fine day set out with a length of rope to try the depths of the cavern. After a drop of five feet they were confronted by a small ledge and a moss encrusted tablet of stone which bore this warning:

Who'er the man that dares this dangerous way,

That wretch no more shall see the light of day,

Shall no more see his children or his wife,

But in this dungeon sob away his life,

Lost in the black oblivion of the gloom,

Here his untimely end and here his tomb.

Ignoring this warning the lads lowered themselves on the rope down the perpendicular side of the cavern until they could stand or crawl, lighting their way by candle. They tied and reeled out a bobbin of thread to mark the way back as a clue, but this soon came to an end and taking the fateful decision to proceed without it had not gone many yards when they saw "summat" which attracted their attention and pressing forward were suddenly plunged into darkness by a drip from the roof which extinguished the candle. Their box of matches then turned out to be damp.

After many hours had gone by and missed by their respective families a search was organised and fortunately at a farm where they had stopped for milk on the way up it was suggested they may have been heading for the cave. Rescuers found the cavern entrance and clambering inside bellowed into the stygian depths as they had discovered the suspended rope.

Clutching one another for warmth in the darkness after an ordeal of 21 hours, mostly spent in fitful sleep, the boys heard the faint yells and returned the calls as best they could and soon rescuers with oil lamps and ropes were dragging them up to the light of day and safety. The 'Mester' of Clough Mill looked at them "dreeply" as they lay gasping and filthy on the grass, tapped his snuff box, took a pinch and asked, "Well, have you had enough?" One of the lads, Billy Bennet, was later to become manager of the mill.

They were probably not the first nor last to have misadventures in the cavern, which is still confidently marked on Ordnance Survey maps, though the entrance is lost. A later writer described the interior as sloping in a northerly direction from Kinder Low End with massive layers of rock and the walls covered in sticky black mud. He recorded that keepers blocked the entrance with timbers and covered them in stones and turf in 1910. However in the 1980s a fissure opened up beside the footpath near the burial mound but this also has since been sealed (it may have been caused by subsidence of the burial mound). A member of Derbyshire Caving Club told the author that a fellow caver had explored the cavern, and that it was very extensive. Edale is on the edge of 'hollow' country with cave rich limestone about a mile away.

One of the keepers who helped cover the entrance in 1910 was a Marriott, the family who originally came to Hayfield in early Tudor times as tenants of the Knights Hospitaller who owned Upper House, Hayfield, on the slopes at Kinder Low End. The Hospitallers had in turn acquired the property from the Knights Templar who might have erected Edale Cross as a boundary marker on land entailed to them by the monks of Basingwerk Abbey.

Both were orders of chivalry dedicated to helping pilgrims and travellers pass safely over difficult and sometimes bandit infested terrain. Both had been founded in Jerusalem, principally to aid Christians in visiting the holy places – the Templars to patrol and protect the pilgrims en route and the Hospitallers to provide hostels, accommodation, and tend the sick. Their story was a dramatic and sad one.

The connection with Kinder started in 1157 when King Henry II was rather unsuccessfully attempting to invade North Wales. He suffered major setbacks when his troops were attacked and routed by the Welsh under Owain Gwynedd as they crossed closely wooded ravines near to the coast in the vicinity of Holywell.

Retreating to a simple motte and bailey castle built by the Earl of Chester close by the Cistercian abbey at Basingwerk he decided to extend the castle and install a garrison of Knights  Templar to protect pilgrims visiting the miraculous holy well of St.Winefred nearby. At the same time he granted the manor of Longdendale and Glossopdale to the abbey to make the presence of the knights more acceptable to them. So pleased was the abbot that he created a chapel in the abbey for the exclusive use of the Templars, which can be seen in the abbey ruins today.

Upper House on the slopes of Kinder

The monks of Basingwerk lost no time in visiting their new manor in the Peak and building a number of roads and causeways to facilitate traffic and trade so their tenants could prosper and pay higher rents and tithes. Monks Road between Charlesworth and Hayfield is one of these, and still has the remains of two medieval cross bases, one known as the Abbot's

Chair beside the road.

It had a continuation now lost across the hillsides to Hayfield and onwards past Oaken Clough and what is now Edale Cross into Edale itself. Whether the monks erected the original cross here at the southern boundary of their manor of Glossopdale, or the Templars after them is unknown. It seems a small preceptory of Templars may have been located at Upper House nearby, (later a farmhouse then shooting lodge). This gave rise to the legend of the 'Champion Cross'- that an aged Templar, a former champion, used to guard pilgrims over the highest portion of the route near Edale Head Cross in expiation of some sin.

Edale medieval roadside cross

The road would then have been visible from near the entrance to the cavern on the hillside which could have acquired an evil reputation as a part-time hiding hole for outlaws waiting to prey on travellers. A similar road crossing high moorland at Blackstone Edge between Lancashire and Yorkshire passed similar features known as Knave Holes, and a preceptory of Hospitallers was situated at the start of its ascent in Butterworth, on what was then a major east west route. An iron cross like a Templar cross was found to have been fixed to the timber gable of this building when it burned down in the 18th century.

The Templars could have been attracted to the Kinder locality for another reason, as what is now the Kinder reservoir was once an area known as Cutlers Green, and it is said iron slag and charcoal cinders from very early iron smelting operations formed heaps near the confluence of the Kinder and William Clough streams.

William Clough was named after 'William le Smith' who in the 1230s illegally cleared forest timber nearby to make charcoal for his smelting operations, without permission from the abbot. He was allowed to continue as a tenant and not only smelted iron but made implements and even blades. It was said that cutlery was manufactured at Hayfield before Sheffield! Mill Hill higher up William Clough was the location of his hammer pond, where a waterwheel drove a giant hammerhead pounding out the heated metal.

It is possible he was smelting bog iron, ironstone or later importing ready made bars.

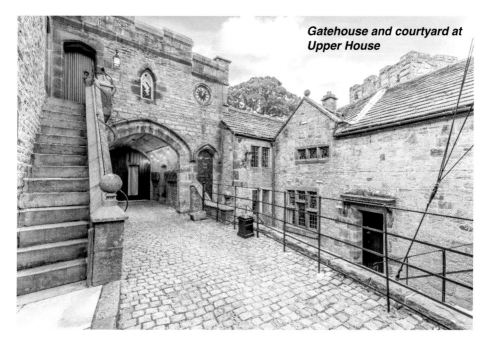

Gatehouse and courtyard at Upper House

Nearby Upper House appears to retain portions of a medieval gatehouse and great hall which could have formed part of the Templar preceptory, with timbers said to be from an old chapel. How it passed to the Hospitallers is part of a tragic story of medieval greed, treachery and envy, triggered by events in the Holy Land.

The Templars were first founded in Jerusalem by nine poor knights sworn to poverty and chastity and a life of protecting pilgrims. In 1120 Baldwin II, the Christian King of Jerusalem, assigned them the Temple Mount as their headquarters and they became known as the 'Poor Knights of Christ of the Temple of Solomon', or Templars for short. Taking monastic vows they agreed to have all in common and their first seal shows two knights riding a single horse.

But soon their fame – they were sworn never to turn back before odds of less than three to one – and success in battle drew recruits from the knightly houses of Europe. After Bernard of Clairvaux, leader of the Cistercian order had praised them they began to receive gifts of land and donations. An air of mystery soon attached itself to the order as they were thought to have found holy relics hidden within secret passages of the Temple Mount, even perhaps the Ark of the Covenant.

At the Council of Troyes in 1127 the Pope freed the order from all local control and taxes, making them answerable only to himself. The knights began to wear their distinctive dress of white mantle and red cross. They shaved their hair but let their beards grow long and regarded bathing as an indulgence! They had sergeants as men-at-arms and squires to look after their horses and weapons who wore darker mantles.

Their first Grand Master, Hugh de Payens went to meet King Henry 1st of England when in Normandy and was sent on a tour of England where the Anglo Saxon Chronicle recorded:

"Hugh of the Temple was received by all good men who gave him presents, and in Scotland also: and by him they sent to Jerusalem much wealth withal in gold and in silver." The Templar shock troops were more than a match for the Saracens. Mounted on heavy chargers they bore down the enemy with long lances, dealing deadly blows with long swords and battle axes. Once, a body of 500 Templar Knights backed by men-at-arms routed a Saracen army of 26,000 men. Unlike most knights they did not expect to be spared if taken in battle and consequently fought to the death.

Their preceptories were set up for older knights to pass on skills to young recruits. Money, arms and horses were gathered and sent on to Jerusalem. They adopted a Saracen system of using coded promissory notes in place of actual cash, which was more risky to transport. Money was deposited with them so they became Europe's first bankers. Soon they had their own fleet of ships and hundreds of castles and manors.

From being poor knights they became very powerful. They helped the Portugese and Spanish kings drive the Moors from Iberia. King Philip IV of France tried to join the order but was turned down.

They had lent him vast sums and he was trying to find a way of not paying it back.

About this time in the 1300s things were going badly in the Holy Land. Jerusalem had fallen and then the last Templar Christian stronghold at Acre fell and the Templars relinquished their hold on Cyprus. Only the Knights Hospitallers held on at Rhodes. Pope Clement suggested a conference to discuss amalgamating the two orders.

But soon after the Templar Grand Master, Jaques de Molay arrived in France to discuss the idea, he and other Templars in the land were arrested on Friday 13th October 1307 (the original 'unlucky' Friday 13th). King Philip and the Pope had decided to get their hands on the Templar wealth.

Painted head found in Templar preceptory

Templars were accused of heresy and illegal practices – spitting on the cross, worshipping a cat or head, performing obscene rituals, acting as priests, giving absolution for sins and condoning sodomy. Under extreme torture some confessed but these forced confessions were later retracted.

What was odd, and made the whole process rather pointless, was the complete lack of money, precious objects, or even horses found at Templar establishments throughout France, or in any other European country, where investigation was made. In England, Edward II reluctantly had them arrested, but then let them go after a brief trial in the church of All Hallows by the Tower in London. In France it was different. Determined to get something for his trouble Philip insisted the Pope condemn the order and seize all their properties.

Since only a few older brothers were found in the preceptories, the able

57

bodied may have left with everything that could be transported. An entire Templar fleet sailed from France for an unknown destination on the day of the arrests. Scotland and Portugal defied the Pope's injunction and ex-Templars were welcome there. The German Templars turned up at the Council of Mainz in full armour and offered to fight anyone who accused them. But King Philip and the Pope pressed ahead and the Order was dissolved in 1312. Two years later De Molay and other leading ex-Templars were sent to the stake for recanting their 'confessions'.

As De Molay, the last Grand Master of the Knights Templar stood facing his grisly end he denied any wrongdoing:

"Not one of us has betrayed his God or his country. I confess my guilt, which was through pain of torture and the fear of death to give utterance to falsehoods, imputing scandalous sins and impurities to an illustrious Order, which hath nobly served the cause of Christianity. I scorn to seek a wretched and disgraceful existence by engrafting another lie on the original falsehood."

Chained to the stake as the flames were kindled he prophesied in a loud voice that both King Philip and Pope Clement would join him before God's Judgement Seat within the year. And so it came about – King Philip was killed in a hunting accident and Pope Clement, who had secretly signed a decree absolving the Order of any wrongdoing, died of a fever.

Pott Shrigley Church and 'cat'

Various theories 'explain' what happened to the Templar treasures. Evidence of worshipping a head or cat remained a puzzle. The head was sometimes said to be three faced! Some Templars said the cat brought fertility to their lands. Inside Pott Shrigley Church on the edge of the moorlands is the medieval image of a grinning Cheshire cat. The church stands on an ancient route through the hills used since Roman times. A mile or two further along at Goyts Bridge, now under Errwood Reservoir, was a hostelry of the Knights of St John and the nearby enclosures were called 'St John's Holding'.

Treasure hunters believe that the reputed money pit on Oak Island in Nova Scotia contains a Templar hoard, transported and hidden there by one or more of their ships, long before Columbus 'discovered' the New World. But there were many more convenient hiding places closer to hand. The quondam caves of Kinder offered secure havens close to an obscure Templar outpost where no-one would dream of looking. Perhaps the mermaid of Kinder really was guarding a treasure?

Kinder Downfall viewed from Sand Heys

In medieval times the High Peak already had some notoriety. Henry of Huntingdon in 1129 wrote of a strange cave, "Cavernis in monte vocato Pec" where a gale blew traveller's clothing aloft and jettisoned it some distance away. This was repeated by Gervase in the following century and went the rounds of the Courts of Europe. The French found it extremely funny that their Norman cousins owned a land where even the mountains farted, and blew their clothes away!

Later writers have identified this with Peak Cavern at Castleton but such a phenomena has never been known there – just a low gurgling from a syphon, rarely heard, has given it the name of Devil's Arse. The wind on Kinder however has no difficulty in snatching clothing, rucksacks and even people, particularly at the Downfall and Kinder Low End.

So how did the preceptory at Upper House, Kinder, come to pass to the Knights Hospitaller? When Edward II followed the Pope's edict to seize the Templar properties in England he delayed for years before eventually handing them over to the Hospitallers, who were patiently waiting to take possession. Many ex-Templars were allowed to join the Hospitallers and there was plenty of time to organise the changeover.

Edale Head roadside cross continues to mark the point near which the path ascends to Kinder Low and the Downfall. It was cast down by Puritans

Medieval style great hall at Upper House

and broken in the 1600s as an object of idolatrous veneration and lay buried for centuries, until the top section was dug up and re-erected by local farmers in 1810. Now it is a protected ancient monument sheltered by stone walls.

The Kinders and Marriotts became the first families to use Upper House purely as tenant farmers. Their house guest Mrs Humphrey Ward wrote a novel set on Kinder entitled the History of David Grieve. Later still the house was adapted as a shooting lodge by a rich Edwardian businessman, James Watts of Abney Hall, Cheadle, who enhanced its medieval architecture and built up a vast collection of antiques. He was a genealogist and spent a lot of time researching his family roots in the medieval period tracing his ancestry back to Norman knights and warlords.

Watts was responsible for the heraldic emblazoning of stained glass windows at Upper House with the coats of arms of his ancestors. Among his many guests was the crime writer, Agatha Christie. Another close friend was the writer and antiquary, Fletcher Moss. The two often made cycling tours in the 1900s, photographically recording old houses and churches for a series of books. Much more recently Upper House has been an exclusive country house wedding venue where its romantic associations with the medieval past has added to a mysterious atmospheric allure. But no-one truly knows the real story of the lonely windswept Champion Cross and the lost caverns of Kinder.

Windy Knoll cave near Mam Tor

Chapter Seven

Outlaws and monsters of the Peak

'All this country is hollow, could you strike it with some gigantic hammer it would boom like a drum'

Sir Arthur Conan Doyle

Mam Tor shivering mountain from Odin Mine

A couple of miles from the southern edges of Kinder Scout lies the last ridge of the moors, Rushup Edge, before the start of the smoother more open limestone country. Here, where the porous limestone meets the impermiable gritstone, mineral rich caves riddle the landscape and streams dive underground through swallow holes.

At one end of the ridge towers Mam Tor, the Mother Mountain, a Celtic name derived from the time when massive earthwork defences which crown the summit with an encircling hillfort was home to people who spoke the old Brythonic tongue. This was a special place to them. On the highest point of Rushup Edge they erected Lord's Seat, a fine lookout and burial place for some ancient chieftain.

Prehistoric bison bones were found near Windy Knoll

This was a place where the upper world met the lower. Where crystalline formations and metal ore in the caves and crags provided both jewels, utensils and tools. Blue John, a rare form of fluorspar is still mined nearby, made into jewellery and ornaments and sold in the shops of Castleton. Silver and lead were once also extracted and smelted into purer forms.

At Windy Knoll, a cave in the reef limestone near the foot of Mam Tor an ancient water hole filled with mud and clay excavated by Victorian geologists revealed the bones of hundreds of extinct animals. Bison, reindeer, bear, wolves, woolly rhino and sabre tooth cat left their remains in the redundant water hole after becoming trapped in a hidden fissure. A bison bone has been radio carbon dated as 37,300 years old!

This was the evocative spot that Sir Arthur Conan Doyle, the creator of Sherlock Holmes, chose to set his spine chilling adventure, "The Terror of Blue John Gap." Dr James Hardcastle is recovering from the effects of tuberculosis and goes to recuperate at a remote Peakland farmhouse. Situated at over 1,300ft, surrounded by limestone crags and caves in the Derbyshire uplands, it is perhaps not the most appropriate spot for a frail patient!

He meets Armitage, a farmer who tells him of the disappearance of sheep which he suspects are being taken and killed by a strange creature from one of the caves. Dr Hardcastle explores an old Roman Blue John mine, which intersects natural caverns leading deep into the underworld, where he hears heavy movements and an unearthly cry.

His curiosity aroused, Dr Hardcastle lies in wait near the mine entrance at night and frozen with terror sees a dark shape pass by against the stars, leaving a colossal footprint in the mud. Shaken, he consults another doctor in a large town nearby, who sends Hardcastle with a note to see a psychiatrist.

Dr Hardcastle confronts the Terror of Blue John Gap

Determined to prove the reality of his story he arms himself with a rifle, enters the cavern and is confronted by the creature.

After he has been missing for some time local villagers find him unconscious and bleeding near the mine entrance. As a precaution they seal the entrance to prevent further misadventures. Hardcastle is sent to a sanatorium where his health deteriorates through his injuries. He writes an horrific account of the antediluvian beast in the depths of the cavern, describing it as a cave bear of gigantic proportions.

He claims he managed to shoot and wound the savage creature before it attacked him. The manuscript is addressed to a sympathetic friend, who passes it on to Conan Doyle after Hardcastle's death. It was published in the Strand magazine in 1910, but the story is generally discounted as the ravings of a dying man. Locals however were more sympathetic to Hardcastle's claim of a vast underground world, populated by dangerous creatures.

The moral of the tale seems to be don't go to recuperate in Derbyshire! However as a qualifying addendum the author would like to offer his own experience in the same locality on a dark night. And unlike Dr Hardcastle I have a witness, who saw the same thing.

In wintertime around the year 2000, after a day delivering boxes of books and magazines to shops, we ended up in the Peak village of Castleton. Heading home along Winnats Pass, a notoriously dark route in winter where the stars stand out clearly above the jagged edges of lofty crags, my young colleague was intrigued to see the dark skies phenomena more closely. So we pulled over near the top, just past the cattle grid and almost opposite to the lonely farm.

I switched off the headlights, leaving on sidelights to warn any approaching traffic, so we could better see the starry sky.

Shortly afterwards what appeared to be a string of torches came jiggling along the road towards us. "Who on earth's that?" I remember puzzling. But my friend had no idea. Whoever or whatever, was now within a few yards of the car.

"Maybe cavers," I suggested tentatively, musing out loud. "Perhaps they're carrying torches about waist height?" Cavers were in the habit of visiting local caves in the evening on this and nearby roads. It hardly matters whether it is dark or light outside a cave when you are plunged into pitchy blackness inside.

Suddenly the 'torches' started to peel off the road to our left, and it became obvious we were looking at pairs of eyes, reflecting the light from our sidelights back at us in the darkness. They seemed to be walking in a line behind one another and each set of eyes disappeared as they turned silently aside towards a solid stone wall until the last pair vanished and the line of lights had gone. But where?

I got out of the car and walked towards where they had been. There was a narrow gate in the drystone wall onto a field, but the bars were too tight to let a lamb through, let alone something which seemed as tall as a mastiff!

Narrow gate into the field where the eyes vanished

There was nothing visible in the field and no sound. Among the possibilities I considered was that it was a vixen leading her foxcubs on a hunting expedition, or that it could have been deer, who travel at night in line one after the other which could have leapt the gate with ease, though we heard no hooves on the metalled road. There was something uncanny in the silence of the manoeuvre and its calm purposefulness, so we didn't linger. The thought of unknown creatures quietly lurking in caves or old mine entrances nearby under those beetling crags was an unnerving one!

Spectacular Winnats Pass near Castleton

I knew that dead bodies had been found in them more than once. An entrance to Winnats Head Cave was near that field.

And not far away two young lovers were robbed and murdered by rough lead miners in the 1750s and their bodies hidden in a mine. A side saddle from the poor girl's horse is exhibited at Speedwell Mine.   Also nearer the bottom of Winnats is Suicide Hole another spot with a sinister legend, where another couple were mysteriously found dead, presumed to have taken their own lives.

This area riddled with caves on the edge of the High Peak has always had a dodgy reputation. Cock Lorel the alleged king of the gypsies in merry Tudor times of Henry the Eighth is said to have supped with the Devil (using a long spoon) in Peak Cavern. The cavern with its 50ft high entrance, the largest in Britain, has been known colloquially as the Devil's Arse since Saxon times. But this occasion may have been an allegorical tale of a meeting with another gypsy king, Giles Hather, at which a language known as thieves cant was first regularised.

When Peveril Castle on its rock above the cavern first fell into decay and ceased to be a prison for those who broke the strict forest laws the gypsies made Castleton their regular endezvous and horse fair. Safe from

The gorge below Peveril Castle leads to Peak Cavern

interference by royal officers they were also in alliance with some of the gentry families nearby, who were once foresters but now broke forest laws themselves.

One such family the Cotterels, were known to have been outlaws in medieval times and it has been suggested Cock Lorel was merely a sly nickname for Cotterel. In the 1330s a Derbyshire gang, specialising in extortion, kidnap and murder, headed by John, James and Nicholas Cotterel were pardoned by Edward III for their 'services' in his Scottish campaign. In 1333 at the battle of Halidon Hill near Berwick Edward III's army, mainly composed of "thieves, murderers and poachers" assisted by some knights and men-at-arms trounced the Scots.

Peak Cavern entrance

Hather, the other gypsy king, is said to have gone about with a hundred followers with painted faces causing havoc wherever he went, terrorising the locality. These rough people who lived and worked in Peak Cavern made rope and twine, very useful articles when things needed tying up – animals, buckets of lead ore for winching up and down in mines, and occasionally travellers

Peveril Castle and Castleton sketched in the 1690s

Horrendous tales tell of hapless visitors to the Peak being robbed and thrown down Eldon Hole, a large natural fissure once believed to reach to the centre of the earth. Around the top was a stone wall which had to be continually renewed as passers by were in the habit of lobbing stones off it down the hole. In Elizabethan times the Earl of Leicester bribed a yokel to be lowered down it in a basket. He was hauled up stark raving mad, and died a few days later in fits without describing what he had seen.

Investigation by potholers in more recent times has revealed that the first mossy shaft is about 200ft deep, with loose stones and bones of sheep and cattle at the bottom, now almost blocking the crawl to another chamber 65ft lower down, but opening out to 90ft high, coated in white flowstone. Above this are large rifts containing numerous stalactites. Blasting at Eldon Hill Quarry has revealed yet another unexplored cave system and smoke was sometimes said to drift into Eldon Hole during quarrying.

Ernest Baker of the Kyndwr club was lowered to the bottom of the Hole in 1900 and described it as: "A grim and gloomy spot lighted by a very small patch of sky. Only parts of the great fissure extending skywards are visible ... the floor is covered by broken stone, falling away rapidly towards the mouth of a dark cave."

Stories of dangerous animals as well as dangerous people persist in this part of the Peak. At Edale on the lower slopes of Kinder Scout people in the lonely farms were alarmed by tales of a creature of enormous size, black, with a voice like a foghorn, which roamed at night baying loudly and strewing the hillsides with dead sheep, their carcasses torn apart.

Collie gone wild – or the last wolf?
A large black carnivore roamed Edale

In October 1925 national papers reported that farmers and police set out armed with rifles and shotguns to hunt the creature without success.

In 1930 a young woman, Greta Shirt of Lee Farm, encountered a large black dog "like a long haired collie" on a moonlit lane near the head of the valley beneath the moors one night. Without any sound the 'dog' merged through the wire fence and was gone. Her father admitted on hearing the tale that he had seen 'a ghost dog' in the same spot, but didn't want to tell her before she was grown up! The lane leads along the old packhorse route past Edale Cross where the Templar once kept his lonely vigil.

The place-name 'booth' in Edale such as Barber Booth and Upper Booth signified an enclosed habitation to keep out wolves which roamed the area. The last wolf was supposed to have been killed at Wormhill not so far away in Tudor times. But has some dark, secretive sub-species yet managed to survive in the cave systems of the Peak, coming out to feed only at night? Perhaps these are the real troglodytes of the moors.

Pennine Way above Edale in winter

More recently in November 1989 armed police and farmers searched Ollerset Moor near Hayfield for a large black predatory animal seen stalking sheep. Known in some places as Black Shuck or Padfoot, the phantom dog is thought to have been an ancient superstition, foreboding coming events. Sightings are associated with the area around Chapel-en-le-Frith, in medieval times a gathering place for Foresters of the Peak who hunted wolves and were paid by the heads collected – hence the old name for an outlaw - 'wolfs head', meaning anyone could take it.

Among outlaws there are associations of Robin Hood in the Hope Valley. His friend and lieutenant, Little John, was buried in Hathersage churchyard, and a bow, cap, and coat of chainmail used to hang in the church. A medieval gravestone of rough hewn gritstone in the porch is said to be his and the Ancient Order of Foresters look after his grave.

The chapel in the forest was built at Chapel-en-le-Frith in 1225 and local tradition avers that Will Scarlett or Scathlock, one of Robin Hood's Merrie Men met his end beside the market cross here in 1284. A square of cobbles near the stocks marks the spot. The town, said to be the capital of the Peak, maintains the medieval tradition of well dressing in the summer, and used to have a bonfire next to the cross on All Hallows Eve.

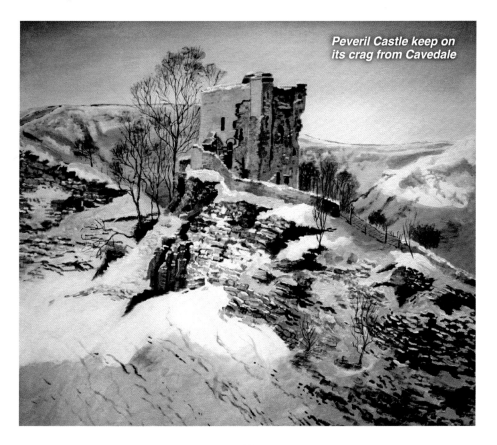
Peveril Castle keep on its crag from Cavedale

An old resident of northern High Peak has eloquently summed up the mystery of the moorlands in describing the feelings of Bonfire Night. "The night on which you had your fire was when the supernatural seemed very close. This was really quite palpable – not just us kids but even the adults felt it.

"There were places you weren't supposed to pass near just then. It was an eerie time – the fireworks, the noise and cheeriness, the Guy burning and fire-jumping. We were all keeping that 'Other' out in the dark. There was a sense of relief when Guy went on the fire. Somehow it was felt that would appease what was out there."

"It had nothing to do with Guy Fawkes, Parliament and 1605, but everything to do with the fields, woods and moors that encompassed us."

Sheer rocky sides of Eldon Hole

Chapter Eight

Screaming skull and bog bodies

Alas Poor Yorick – I knew him Horatio, a fellow of infinite jest...
here hung those lips that I have kissed...

Shakespeare's Hamlet

Superstitious cults about heads probably originate from the primitive display of hunting trophies by our earliest human ancestors.

The Templars were said to consult a 'talking head' whose eyes flashed fire. In one version of the medieval 'Quest for the Holy Grail' the Grail Castle turned out to contain a talking head, not a cup from the Last Supper. But cups were sometimes made of human skulls and the Vikings drank from the skulls of their slain enemies. 'Guardians of the Old Ways' hid stone heads in Longdendale to protect wells. And carved stone faces on houses and in walls occur throughout the Pennines. The ancient Celts worshipped the human head as the seat of soul and kept trophies of their enemies. The British king, Bran the Blessed, decapitated in Ireland, kept talking to his followers for years afterwards until they buried his head on Tower Hill, London – as a Guardian against invaders.

Screaming skulls seem to fall into this head cult category. They have miraculous powers to interfere with current events, so have to be respected and looked after, otherwise misfortune may strike. If treated well they bring good luck and must never leave their chosen location. There are several lonely farmhouses around the Peak moors reputedly with disarticulated human craniums in niches, on window ledges, or walled up...

Nearly four thousand years ago early on a warm summer's day a procession plodded up a steep and verdant green hillside from the valley bottom and halted just at the edge of rough pasture beneath a ridgeway. Here an area of turf had been freshly cut into a wide circle and the turf piled up around the edges. Big stones had been laid against the earthen bank to hold it in place. This was the beginning of Cadster stone ring cairn and a folk tale persisting to the present day.

A young woman who lay on a rustic hurdle strewn with flowers drawn by two white oxen, was reverently carried to the centre of the circle. A small bundle was placed against her breast by a young bearded man. A fine black hunting dog stood by his side, its tail drooping with sadness. At the poignant moment of placing his dead infant on the mother's cold breast the man raised his hand to his face and wept.

Then he produced a knife which flashed gold in the sun and slit the dog's throat. It yelped, but he held it reverently and it looked into his face as he muttered words and it gently lay down and died. He placed the faithful animal at her feet and a patch of blood soaked into the russet soil.

An elderly white robed Druid began to intone his hymn of invocation to the spirits of the hill, earth and trees, to the winds, the rain and the sun and to old gods of the underworld to welcome their daughter and bring her safely to the place where coldness was warmth, wet was dry and darkness was light – the ancestral Summerland.

The people laid gifts around her, cups of food and drink and small utensils for use on her journey. Children added little bunches of wild flowers. The priest sang a song in which the people joined, asking that their sister smile and be happy and keep a watchful eye on the fruitfulness of the land.

She and the dog who accompanied her were to join the ancestors to be guardians of the place forever.

A Bronze Age funeral at Cadster ring cairn

There are several lost burial cairns on the side of Ladder Hill near Tunstead Milton visible on Lidar (aerial mapping) around Tunstead Farm, long known for a curious relic once kept in the farmhouse.

No-one could really say where the skull of 'Dickie' came from, but a lot of stories to account for 'him' have been told and re- told, so there's no harm in repeating them. But first lets consider the most likely origin.

It has long been a superstition throughout the Peak and elsewhere that an old skull, found in a burial mound untouched by the ancestors for thousands of years, which was finally being robbed and demolished to provide stones for walling the fields, should be taken into the farmhouse and kept as a good luck token. Similar skulls with such origins are known to have existed at Flagg Hall near Buxton and Dunscar Farm near Castleton.

During intensive clearing and dividing of fields when the old Forest of the Peak was "land grabbed" by gentry and sitting tenants from the 1500s onwards, particularly after the plundering of church lands by Henry VIII in the 1530s, antiquarian trophies once hidden and venerated were continually turning up.

The Derbyshire Monuments record for Cadster stone circle burial cairn states that the circle, "may have been the origin of a skull known as 'Dickie'." It may well have been Cadster, or one of the others nearby, for this was a fruitful valley in Bronze Age and Neolithic times, when farming was carried on at higher levels in the Peak even without fertilizers thanks to better temperatures and a kinder climate than today. Local historians have

A slight ring and heel stone directly to the south – all that remains of Cadster ring cairn

already suggested that the skull once kept at Tunstead was from a plundered burial cairn nearby. But for hundreds of years locals believed two different stories which don't really tie in with the apparitions seen on the hillsides and in the farmhouse.

The spirit of a girl is seen not only at Tunstead but also at Cadster the next hamlet along the valley, "like a white shirt floating in the breeze". A tenant farmer at Tunstead many years ago saw her bending over the cradle of his sick child. Both places were probably part of the Bronze Age community which once inhabited the area. A largish black dog frequently appears and was mentioned by local writer S.O.Addy in 1895 and also local Combs residents Crichton Porteous and Margaret Bellhouse who herself saw the black dog.

"This dog appears from nowhere at the top of the hill on the road to Combs and walks behind one right down the hill when coming dusk. It acknowledges no-one, makes no sound and disappears at the bottom of the lane,"she wrote.

Local people believed that the dog haunted 'Dickie's land' and was best avoided after dark as it was a guardian spirit. The dog is sometimes seen across the valley at Ollerenshaw and the hamlet of Cockyard beside Combs Reservoir, which was built to feed the Peak Forest Canal in the 18th century.

Most likely the skull was recovered when rubble was being taken from a burial cairn on the hill to extend stone walls.

Skulls are the hardest bones of the body and along with thigh bones tend to be the only parts that remain after a long interment. Placed in the farmhouse as a good luck token its true origin would soon be forgotten and various tales invented.

The most famous is that it was the head of Ned Dickson or Dixon a soldier who had been away fighting in wars of religion in France during the 1590s. Returning home at last he found that cousins had taken possession of his patrimony, believing him to be dead. Invited to stay and discuss their common conundrum he was murdered by his avaricious relatives, but they were then plagued with bad luck until his skull was dug up and brought into the farmhouse on the advice of a local witch. It didn't work.

Firstly the woman was killed by a blow from her husband and then the man was crushed by a falling oak tree on the farm. But any attempt to remove the skull was met by pandemonium, weeping and moaning, furniture creaking and moving, and ornaments being smashed.

At one point the skull was buried in consecrated ground but that didn't stop the ill luck. Animals died, crops failed and accidents happened on the farm, so it was brought back. It was flung onto a midden heap, but set up an outraged screaming, rolled to the front door and tapped against it to be let in! Once it was thrown into Combs Reservoir, but all the fish started to die and they had to fish it out. It was walled up on the farm and for a while all went well. Then house renovations revealed it again and the surprised new owners placed it on a window sill to continue to look out over 'Dickie's land'.

Dickie's skull on 1900s postcard

A learned doctor who examined the relic in the early 1800s pronounced it to be the skull of a young woman of about 18 years of age.

This tied in a bit more with the second, less popular story, that it belonged originally to a co-heiress whose sister murdered her for love of a young man and the farm. Whilst being murdered she had time to say that unless she got her share by never leaving the farm she would curse the place and the marriage. Perhaps they misunderstood her meaning, but her head was then displayed in a niche. Could have been awkward when the vicar came to tea to discuss nuptials? All this murdering seems to have gone on without anyone being hanged.

By this time the skull was getting worse for wear. In postcards of the 1900s it is shown as basically just the top, rear, and base of the cranium, with no frontal features at all. Finally these were in three pieces and by the 1960s, when Clifford Rathbone a local journalist visited the farm, even these had disappeared.

Most of the later farmers at Tunstead revered the skull and believed that it protected the farm. They would not speak ill of it and refused to move the relic from its habitual position on an upstairs window ledge, although some accounts say the kitchen.

"If you were good to Dickie and didn't say stupid things about him he was good to you," said one farmer. He even believed that Dickie opened and closed gates for him on the drive, warned him about animals that were in trouble, looked after crops and warded off burglars and thieves. Dickie looked after the farm and was more valuable than his best cow!

Tunstead Farm on old postcard

But Dickie's main triumph and claim to fame was when 'he' nearly stopped the London and North Western Railway Company in its tracks. Travellers on the Manchester/Buxton commuter train today may not realise they are traversing "Dickie's land" in the valley between Whaley Bridge and Chapel en le Frith stations. They are travelling beneath a bridge which 'Dickie' repeatedly demolished and along a trackbed which continually sank into supernatural quicksands and slime! Although, these problems might have something to do with the enlargement of nearby Combs Reservoir in 1840, which raised the earthen embankment to contain an extra few thousands gallons of water and made adjacent land more waterlogged. But locals firmly believed it was all down to Dickie's skull.

Deeply conservative in a traditional sense, the skull disapproved of this new-fangled mode of transport and the rough navvies who came digging and hammering, damning and blasting, all over the sacred valley.

After repeated disasters the line was moved, a new access road was made and the bridge had to be re-located. The navvies themselves being rather superstitious had downed tools and refused to work at one point. It was a dangerous enough job anyway, without supernatural interference in the work!

So famous were the occurrences that national papers picked up the story and a local dialect poet Samuel Laycock celebrated this David v. Goliath (or skull v. railway) encounter in a poem published by the Buxton Advertiser in 1870.

Neaw,Dickie,be quiet wi'thee lad?
An' let navvies an' railways be;
Mon, tha shouldn't do soa, it's too bad,
What harm are they doin' to thee?
Deod folk shouldn't meddle at o'
But leov o'these matters to th'wick;
They'll see they're done gradely, aw know-
Dos't 'yer what aw say to thee, Dick?

The arrow shows 'Dickie's' bridge on the railway

No-one looks at their best when they've been in a bog for a couple of thousand years. Cheshire's Lindow Man certainly didn't, but he looked a lot better than most of his contemporaries. Bogs are acid rich and oxygen poor, preserving organic matter like skin and clothing which normally decays underground, but often destroying bones, which survive in other environments.

About a thousand reasonably well preserved bog bodies have been found throughout Britain and Europe, and the oldest are over 2,000 years of age. But the very first known were uncovered right here in the Peak District.

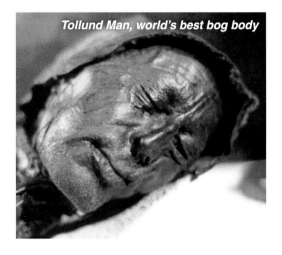
Tollund Man, world's best bog body

There is a tradition of losing folk in the Peak District. 'Lost Lad' above Ladybower is a beauty spot and magnet for sturdy ramblers, but few now recall the sad event which led to the naming of the place. A boy called Abraham Lowe looked after his widowed mother and their farm near the now drowned village of Derwent.

Long before Ladybower Reservoir filled the valley they made a precarious living from sheep farming on the extensive moorland pasture. One winter's day he set out to bring some to lower levels with his faithful sheepdog, but a blizzard enveloped the pair beyond Back Tor, at a spot where there is very little shelter from the icy blast.

Cast away in a snowstorm he managed to scratch "Lost Lad" on a rock with a stone before succumbing to hypothermia, along with his faithful canine friend. Months later their wizened remnants were found by a passing shepherd. Even now, occasionally in wintertime walkers still report seeing the pair briefly before they abruptly fade away.

There is also the story of a farmer who similarly perished on these moors, and his faithful sheepdog stayed by him somehow surviving until the Spring, when it was found alive much the worse for its ordeal but succumbed soon after. Further along Cut Gate track towards Langsett there is another 'Lost Lad' marked on the map but probably there are many such tales of these bleak moors.

A man and a woman cast away in a stowstorm near the Salt Cellar, Derwent Edge, in January 1674

The first true bog bodies of the Peak known were discovered centuries earlier than this, at a spot not far away from Lost Lad. Again tragedy had struck in a snowstorm when a couple who dealt in cattle travelled over the high moors to Derwent from nearby Bradfield.

"These two persons were lost in a great snow on the moors, in the Parish of Hope, near The Woodlands, in Derbyshire, January 14th 1674 and not being found until May 3rd following, the snow lasting the greater part of that time, they smelt so strongly the coroner ordered them to be buried on the spot." So wrote Dr Charles Balguy in the Transactions of the Royal

Society in 1734, as his account of -"The dead bodies of a man and a woman preserved 49 years in the moors of Derbyshire."

Derwent Hall from an old postcard before it was demolished and drowned

Dr Balguy was a Derbyshire man, born at Derwent Hall in 1708 and had grown up with a story which was well known in the district. Later qualifying as a medical doctor he submitted the account to the learned society of which he was a member.

"They lay in the peat moors 28 years nine months before they were looked at again, when some countrymen, having observed the qualities of this soil of preserving dead bodies from corrupting, were curious to open the ground to see, and they found them in no way altered, the colour of their flesh being fair and natural and as soft as newly dead people. They were afterwards exposed as a spectacle for 20 years, though much changed in that time by being so often uncovered.

"In 1716 their condition was as follows: The man perfect, his beard strong, about a quarter of an inch long, the hair of his head short, his skin hard and of a tanned leather colour, pretty much the colour of the earth they lay in.

"The woman by some rude people had been taken completely out of the ground to which one may impute her greater decay; one leg was off, the flesh decayed, the bone sound; on her face the upper lip and tip of her nose decayed, but nowhere else. Her hair was long and springy like that of a living person.

"They had lain about a yard deep in the soil or moist moss, but without any water in the place. When their stockings were drawn off, the man's legs which had never been uncovered before, were quite fair, the flesh when pressed with the finger pitted a little and the joints moved freely, other parts were much decayed.

"What was left of their clothes (for people had cut bits off) was firm and good, the woman had on a piece of good serge which seemed never the worse."

Another account was written by historian, Fletcher Moss, who gives a letter written by the local clergyman, the Rev. S. Wormald, curate of the village. Seemingly a descendant of the tragic pair had prevailed on him to decently bury them.

"When I lived at Derwent in 1724 I buried them at Hope. I saw them dug up and put in coffins and I do affirm those parts of ye body that had never been exposed to ye air were as entire and firm as when they were lay'd in. They had lain in ye moss 28 years and then been exposed every summer to the view of people who came out of curiosity for 20 years, which makes in ye whole 48 years. They were laid in ye moss 23 years before I was born and yet I buried them. This is a matter of fact. Ye joints were pliable and ye hands and nails perfect."

Curiosity did not leave them alone even in the churchyard at Hope as they were looked at again in another 20 years and found to have decayed in the normal course of nature, the ordinary soil of the valley floor not having the preservative properties found in acidic peat bogs.

Doubtless the peat bogs still hold their secrets. Along with Mesolithic hunter-gatherers and perhaps even other prehistoric denizens of this wild region, the bodies of more recent victims may lie preserved.

The Derwent valley has seen other strange comings and goings. It once housed "Tin Town" home to thousands of navvies and their families working on the series of masonry dams for the reservoirs. Houses built of corrugated iron lined with wood and heated by open fires fronted properly laid streets in serried rows on the hillsides at Birchinlee. There was a school for the children, a pub, a recreation ground, community hall/cinema and even a police station!

It took 12 years to finish the first dam up the valley at Howden and three more to complete Derwent Dam which opened in 1915 as WW1 raged in Europe. Then the navvies began to move on to other projects and the town which had raised a generation of children was bulldozed.

The next town to get the chop was Derwent itself and the village of Ashopton on the main Snake road at the foot of the valley. In 1940 bodies from the churchyards of both villages were dug up and reburied at Bamford further down the valley.

When the Ladybower Dam was completed in 1944 and the villages fully flooded the spire of Derwent Woodlands church was left poking out of the waters

The Ladybower Reservoir (the largest in England) has drowned the church of Derwent to supply water to Sheffield, Derby, Nottingham and Leicester.

as a memorial to the lost village. The medieval packhorse bridge opposite Derwent Hall, built by monks, was removed and reassembled at Slippery Stones at the head of the valley, where it still is. Derwent Hall itself, the birthplace of Dr Balguy who was a descendant of the Norman foresters of Hopedale, was lost beneath the reservoir. Its shattered ruins can be seen occasionally at times of drought along with what is left of the church. In 1947 the church spire too was dynamited as it had become dangerous.

It is a pity that the fine old hall dating from 1672 was lost. It was said to have been built by a Balguy who was successful as a lawyer. He packed so many gold coins end-on in boxes that they could not be prised out! Finally passing to the Duke of Norfolk who used it as a shooting lodge, Derwent Hall eventually went to pay death duties on the Duke's vast holdings and became one of the earliest Youth Hostels for the burgeoning ramblers movement in the 1930s before Ladybower was built. Many youthful memories of freedom in the fresh air of the hills were first made here by young workers from smoky Sheffield and Manchester.

Ladybower viewed from White Tor Derwent Edge

Bogs are strange things, on occasion they burst and flow in a terrifying liquid deluge like a Tsunami smashing and drowning everything in their path! This happened most famously at Crow Hill above Haworth on Sept 2nd 1824 when three of the Bronte children, Branwell, Anne and Emily had gone for a walk on the moors.

Their father Patrick, Curate at Haworth Church, peered out of an upstairs window late in the afternoon for signs of them returning and saw instead a darkening sky above the moor and then lightning with a colossal thunderclap, followed by an earth tremor which shook the parsonage. Another witness, James Mitchell of Oldfield House recorded the weather was hot and sultry. "The western clouds changed to the colour of new sheet copper, from which issued vivid lightning with a tremendous single peal of thunder."

A torrential downpour enveloped the moors and suddenly the whole mass of peat and heather on Crow Hill erupted and started to move. It knocked down trees, bowled over stone walls, smashed bridges in the brook and slithered downhill towards the River Worth. A lone walker frantically waved a warning to a group of children who ran terrified for the nearest farmhouse, believed to be Ponden Hall, where Patrick Bronte found Branwell, Anne and Emily cowering in the porch.

Bog bursts are quite well known in Ireland and the remote fastnesses of Scotland and are caused by a sudden build up of water in the peat moss, which becomes destabilized and begins to slide over the bedrock beneath. In the Peak there is evidence of a similar occurrence at Red Brook on Kinder Scout in a storm some time during the late 19th century.

Ernest Baker recorded in 1903: "This spot a few years ago vied with the Downfall's rugged gorge in grandeur of rock scenery ... Observe this notable object lesson in the rapidity with which the face of nature is altered. The scarps are smoothed away, the jagged boulders entombed and the deep ravine well nigh filled up by the movements of the peat moss and the growth of vegetation, chiefly bilberry and ling. Some photographs I have of this once rocky clough would be unrecognisable now."

A final moors mystery I might just end with is the strange case of the re-appearing deer. In 1640 owing to pressure from tenants whose properties were being damaged, King Charles 1st decreed that all red deer should be destroyed or removed from the Royal Forest of the Peak. However there are today large wild herds at Longshaw near Hathersage and a sizeable one in the Goyt Valley near Buxton – whether escapes from deer parks, or remnants of the original herd no-one quite knows.

Epilogue

There are so many mysteries unknown or waiting to be discovered in the moorlands of the central Peak District I am confident that many more books could be written.

If you like this subject I recommend the work of David Clarke and Andy Roberts who have investigated and collected many folktales which make up the fabric of local lore. Dr. David Clarke runs courses on Media and Folklore at Sheffield Hallam University and is a regular contributor to Fortean Times a celebrated monthly magazine about unusual phenomena.

Experts in their own field on ancient monuments, archaeology, history and trackways of the Peak include the Dodds who investigated ancient roads and Neville Sharpe who compiled a classic guide to medieval crosses, both published by the late lamented Landmark series of books.

I am a local historian and my principal interest in writing about mysterious folklore is to find any historical factual basis of the tales and to try to link objective reality with what may otherwise appear to be the spurious imaginings of witnesses. Where the two parts join we have an interesting story. And occasionally I have managed to turn up fresh information!

There are probably two main sorts of attitude to books of this kind. The enthusiast for supernatural stories is naturally interested and sympathetic. The sceptic may pick up such a book by accident and laugh. But there remains a substantial body of open minded people whose opinions have not yet been set in stone. I hope this brief offering may provide some enjoyable food for thought. It contains some tales not previously told. Naturally there is an element of Gothic horror. Folk frequently prefer sensation to sentiment.

I will just add – if you decide to venture forth and visit any of the places mentioned – do take care, lest...

Like one that on a lonesome road
Doth walk in fear and dread,
And having once turned round walks on,
And turns no more his head;
Because he knows, a frightful fiend
Doth close behind him tread.

Samuel Taylor Coleridge – Rime of the Ancient Mariner

Heathery moors looking towards Carl Wark Iron Age fort and the Hope Valley. Carl Wark is an enigmatic defensive structure built with enormous five foot blocks of gritstone. Who were its builders frightened of in the prehistoric past? Excavations at a similar promontory fort a few miles south at Fin Cop revealed the massacred remains of women and children, tumbled into a ditch then buried with masonry from the defences. Their fears were clearly not groundless.

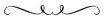

Acknowledgements

First and foremost I would like to acknowledge the help of artist, historian and geologist, David Kelsall, (DK) for his invaluable encouragement and agreeable company on several expeditions into darkest Peakland. His suggestions for research material and his superb illustrations enhance the final product.

Many writers left tracks in the sand which I have followed for some of the way. In addition, online research now makes accessing rare publications and information an easier task. But apart from looking at the older published sources there is no substitute for actually visiting the places, getting a feel for them, taking photographs and talking to people! Material from museums, private collections and archives is most valuable.

Modern writings which I have mentioned include those by northern authors David Clarke and Andy Roberts, Roly Smith, Ron Collier and the superb website compiled by Steve Lewis of New Mills. Many older writers I have referred to in the text are well worth looking up. If I have missed anyone, I apologise in advance.

Wormstones, Chunal Moor, where a dragon was said to wind his scaly coils

Index